Trading Your Worry for Wonder

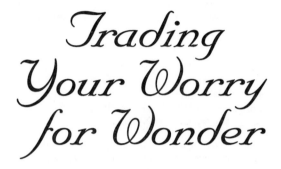

Trading Your Worry for Wonder

A WOMAN'S GUIDE TO OVERCOMING ANXIETY

Cheri Fuller

BROADMAN
& HOLMAN
PUBLISHERS
Nashville, Tennessee

Published by Broadman & Holman Publishers, Nashville, Tennessee
Acquisitions & Development Editor: Janis Whipple
Interior Design: Leslie Joslin
Published in association with the literary agency of Alive Communications,
Inc., 1465 Kelly Johnson Blvd., Suite 320, Colorado Springs, CO 80920

4261-92
0-8054-6192-2

Dewey Decimal Classification: 152.4
Subject Heading: FEAR / WOMEN / WORRY
Library of Congress Card Catalog Number: 96-9144

Library of Congress Cataloging-in-Publication Data
Fuller, Cheri.
        Trading your worry for wonder : a woman's guide to
overcoming anxiety / Cheri Fuller.
                p.   cm.
        ISBN 0-8054-6192-2
        1. Christian women—Religious life. 2. Fear—Religious aspects—
Christianity. I. Title.
BV4527.F85   1996
248.8'43—dc20   96-9144
                                                        CIP

96 97 98 99 00 5 4 3 2 1

This book is dedicated to my daughter, Alison. In nineteen years you have brought us so much joy! Through your life and faith, God has truly filled me with wonder and gratitude. The adventurous spirit with which you pursue life and the passion with which you seek God inspire me to press on to follow Him. As you launch out in God's purpose for your life with this generation of young men and women, I pray you'll run the race with trust and joy, remembering:

> "The LORD your God is with you,
>   he is mighty to save.
> He will take great delight in you,
>   he will quiet you with his love,
>   he will rejoice over you with singing."
>
> ZEPHANIAH 3:17

Acknowledgments

Many women in my life have graciously contributed to this book, and I am most grateful for their prayers, stories, and counsel: Melanie Hemry, Cathy Herndon, Pam Whitley, Louise Tucker Jones, Pat Fuller, Lynn Parsley, Cynthia Morris, Cyndi Lamb, Linda Leddy, Esther Heritage, Maisie Bross, Peggy Stewart, and Flo Perkins. And to all the women who were willing to share their stories with me, I thank you from the bottom of my heart.

A sincere thank-you to Broadman & Holman Publishers and especially my editor, Janis Whipple, for her editorial skills and insights. Janis, you were a joy to work with! To my agent, Greg Johnson at Alive Communications, many thanks for your encouragement, vision, and support of this project. To Keith Miller and Bruce Larsen, whose book *The Edge of Adventure* helped us put into words and action what we felt God leading us to do and spurred us on in living the Great Adventure with Jesus Christ. And most of all, thank you, Holmes, for standing with me in your patient, loving way these twenty-seven years together as God turned my worry into wonder! I couldn't ask for a better husband and life partner, and I love you.

Contents

Introduction

Do you love me, or do you not?
You told me once, but I forgot. . . .

As my son lay sleeping in an oxygen tent in his hospital bed beside me, I gazed for what seemed like hours at monotonous gray walls, faded cowboy curtains, and drab construction-paper bells left over from Christmases past. I moved restlessly around in the brown vinyl chair, trying to get comfortable, but sleep wouldn't come.

"Trust God; everything will work out OK," one of the nurses said when I asked if Justin would be able to go home for Christmas. *Trust who?* I thought as I sat there alone by the window. We'd had everything planned. The tree at home was decorated with twinkle lights and homemade ornaments; the boys' stockings I'd worked on for months were finally finished. My parents-in-law were coming into town to celebrate the holiday weekend with us.

We had brought Justin into Saint John's with a severe asthma attack two days before; but his breathing was better now, and he wanted to go home so badly. We were newcomers in the city and had no friends in town. We hadn't had a visitor, except for the minister from a local church who told me

1

before even sitting down that he really didn't like hospitals and surely I didn't mind his leaving before too long. The hospital was a lonely place anytime, but especially at Christmas.

The whole experience had been a nightmare from the minute we walked in the emergency room. Justin's doctor was out of town. I hated seeing him held down by nurses while being stuck several times to insert an IV in his arm. Now he was pricked and poked hourly. And instead of sitting on Santa's knee sharing his Christmas wish or hanging his stocking on the mantelpiece, there he was stuck in a drab hospital, hooked up to an IV, and caged by an oxygen tent. *But surely we'll get to take him home on Christmas Eve. The nurse told me they're sending all the kids home they can.*

The next morning Justin's doctor stopped by on his rounds and then called me out into the hall. "I'm sorry, Mrs. Fuller, but your son still needs to be on IV fluids. It's just too soon to send him home."

My earlier worry about his asthma had turned to frustration and now into full-blown anger. The family called to say they'd just wait to come celebrate Christmas until Justin got out of the hospital. Until then, they told us, just act as if Christmas hadn't yet arrived.

That would be easy, I thought. *There's no tree in the room; we haven't brought up any presents.* I tried to look cheerful as I explained the plan to Justin.

"Mimi and Pop thought it would be so much more fun to celebrate at home than here at the hospital. So they're just going to play like Christmas is the day you get out. They want us to wait too."

"No Christmas stockings? No opening presents tomorrow morning?" he asked as his face fell. I didn't even have a car there to go get his stocking. My husband, Holmes, had to be at home with our eighteen-month-old Christopher, so it looked like it was going to be a long evening. I opened a book to read him a story, and then his dinner arrived.

After Justin's dinner tray was removed, a man brightly dressed as Santa came bounding down the hall calling, "Merry Christmas!"

It is anything but a merry Christmas, I thought. He stopped in Justin's room and delivered a cowboy hat, just his size. As I watched Santa continue down the hall delivering presents, I asked the nurse with some skepticism, "Did some organization send this gift as a yearly project?" thinking it must be a good deed of Kiwanis or Rotary Club.

"Oh, no," she replied. "Several years ago a couple's only daughter who was three years old died in this ward on Christmas Eve. Now each year the parents find out the exact size of each child and have the gifts delivered by Santa so they can remain anonymous. They know what it's like to be here."

Moments later, two little Camp Fire girls brought in a handmade white felt mitten ornament, decorated with holly, and presented it to Justin. "Merry Christmas!" they chimed as they continued happily down the hall.

Hardly had their words faded away when a family of Mexican-American carolers arrived. Gaily dressed in red and green native costumes, guitars in hand, they sang "Silent Night" and concluded their carol-singing with "Joy to the World."

And we were going to put off Christmas.

A short while later, a big University of Oklahoma football player in his varsity jersey strolled in and began to chat with our son. An avid football fan, Justin couldn't believe that a "real live" gridiron hero had come just to see him. He was even more amazed when the burly athlete produced a surprise gift for him.

"A cowboy rifle and spurs!" he exclaimed. "They go with my hat!"

The "coincidence" took my breath away.

The next day, on Christmas morning, a tall, thin man quietly entered the room and sat on the edge of the bed. Like some character from a Dickens novel, his clothes were worn. Without a word, he took out an old flute and began to play a lovely Christmas medley. One carol blended into another as the simplicity of each song took on a beauty beyond any I had ever known. Finishing his serenade, he handed Justin a small cup full of tiny red candies. Then with a smile, he slipped out the door.

Slowly but clearly, I began to realize that none of the people who had shared their love and gifts with us knew us or had even told us their names. We had done nothing to earn or deserve their gifts. While my own pain from the past had created a cold barrier around my heart, these simple acts of kindness caused the walls of hurt and disappointment to crack. Soon, I knew, they would fall.

That lonely hospital, with its noisy bustle and antiseptic smells, became a place of God's healing love. Away from family, friends, and our baby son, without our tree or traditions, God had delivered His special gift.

God loved me. I sensed it for the first time in many years.

God at a Distance

It's hard to trust someone if you're not sure he loves you. It's hard to jump in the arms of a daddy when you don't know if he'll be there to catch you. *Do you love me, or do you not? You told me once, but I forgot.* I had forgotten that God loved me. Not sure He listened or even cared. I went through the motions, showed up for church, tried to do all the right things. But I kept God at a distance. And inside, I was so afraid. How did I get that way?

Small World

I grew up in a very protected environment—in a big city, but a very small world. My mother didn't drive, so our territory consisted of home, yard, church, and, after age seven, school. We walked almost everywhere we went, chaperoned by Mom or my big sisters. And on Sundays Papa dropped us at church and occasionally on summer nights drove us to the ice cream store. Papa, twelve years older than Mom, thought a mother of six belonged at home, not driving around Dallas with kids in the back of the car!

Mama worked hard to make a home for the six of us children. As the youngest of five children, she'd grown up in a chaotic home during the depression, with her alcoholic, unemployed father and two brothers—while her mother traveled with her dancing twin sisters to support the family. Mama was determined her home was going to be different. She sewed all of the clothes for five daughters—beautiful pinafores and five matching Easter dresses every year. She cooked big meals, served at the same time each day while Papa went to work at the insurance company. Mom never went to bed until all clothes, towels, and diapers were clean, folded, and put neatly away.

At home I learned obedience (a big value at our house), how to read, a strong work ethic, and a competitive spirit, for with five girls in a row there was lots of sibling rivalry. There was also plenty of singing, playing games, and going to church. But I also learned and internalized a lot of fear. Experts believe that being raised in an overprotective home can contribute to chronic anxiety or even panic disorder in adult life. In addition, a one-time traumatic event or experiencing significant losses in childhood can predispose a person to anxiety.[1] I had both factors.

We have family jokes about why we never visited the zoo. "One of you might have gotten loose and been snatched by an animal," we were told. Mama was also afraid of big storms, tornadoes, airplanes, poverty, and many other things. One of her sources of pride was that she had gotten all of us through childhood with not one broken bone. One of her brothers died of blood poisoning in childhood after being hit by a truck, and her other brother developed grand mal epilepsy when he fell backward off their high front porch. Mom was determined nothing was going to happen to any of her children and did all she could to protect us.

I can still hear her voice, "Don't climb that tree! You might fall and break something!" So we made mudpies under the big persimmon tree in the backyard instead of adventuring up the branches.

"Don't swim to the deep part of the pool—you might drown!" I heard even after we'd taken swimming lessons. My aunt drowned when I was ten years old, confirming that fear. My closest grandfather had died shortly before her death. And then a year later, when I was eleven years old and about to start sixth grade, my father died in the middle of the night of a heart attack, his fourth in several years.

A few days later, the six of us sat around mother in the long black limousine. Dressed in our Sunday best, cheeks streaked with tears, we watched as the long procession of cars began its slow journey from the red brick church to Restland Cemetery, where Papa would be buried. I was stunned by our loss and felt as if my world had fallen apart.

In contrast, other people bustled by, hurrying places in the September sunshine. Cars loaded with businessmen, mothers, and laughing children sped down the highway. They didn't even take time to glance at our procession. Their lives were going on, and mine had seemed to stop.

Life was never the same.

Unable to Trust

We moved after the school year. My two oldest sisters left home, still teenagers, when Mom remarried a year and a half later.

At age twelve, I gave my life to Christ and will never forget the pastor's words when I came up out of the baptismal waters, "You are raised to walk in newness of life!" I knew I needed a Savior. And I wanted to walk in "newness of life," but the old fears and questions dragged me down throughout adolescence—questions about whether heaven and hell were real, whether God really cared and heard my prayers, and if life made any sense at all. Like many children who lose a parent in childhood, I felt abandoned. Why had Papa died when we all prayed for him to be well? Trusting anyone was difficult after that—especially God.

I'll never forget that sunny spring morning when I was thirteen. Saturdays were my favorite day of the week—so packed full of promise and fun. I sat at the breakfast table eating Mama's silver dollar pancakes and planning my afternoon.

Two of my best friends, Lyn and Bill, and I were going to a movie that evening. I still had morning chores to do while Lyn and Bill returned from a hunting trip at Lyn's grandfather's farm.

The shrill ring of the telephone shattered my peace. "Cheri," I heard, "there's been an accident. Bill and Lyn were cleaning their guns. . . . Lyn is dead."

I froze, trying to understand. It felt like the world turned upside down and I couldn't find my place. Lyn, study partner, movie companion . . . only thirteen, dead.

Lyn wasn't the only one to die that morning. The last remnants of trust were blown out of my life with that blast.

The world was a dangerous, deadly place. My fears spun out of control; but I carefully stuffed them down as I pressed on through high school and college, staying busy with dating, drill team, and making A's.

So years later, as a twenty-nine-year-old mother of two, when our son's asthma attacks hit our life, the fear I'd carried so long—fears of losing someone I loved, fears about death and sickness, doubts about whether God cared, whether it really mattered to pray—came to the surface. Like the child who said to her mom, "I'll do it myself," I'd tried to handle life on my own, without God, but it was becoming too much for me.

The Number One Problem—Fear

A recent survey of more than fifteen thousand Christians by a major ministry organization showed that fear is the number one problem of women. Maybe you don't have the fears I had, but what are the fears and anxieties that hamstring women's lives?

Like me, many mothers worry about the health of their children. Many women fear for their children and teens and the world they are growing up in. One friend I know hopes and prays for the rapture before her boys go into their teen years. There is a fear of letting go of control. Moms of teenagers are often afraid their adolescents may get involved with alcohol, drugs, or the wrong crowd.

In the 1990s, health concerns, such as cancer (especially breast cancer), are prominent among things women worry about. Some fear success because of the role conflict it would cause with their mates and their priorities as mothers. Still others fear that they cannot make it financially on their own if their marriages fail or their husbands are laid off. Singles say, "I'm afraid I'm going to lose my job, and I have no one to depend on," or "I'm afraid I'll lose my friend; I continually fear loneliness."

And recent happenings, such as the Oklahoma City bombing, cause women to fear the unknown, the future, or disasters. Overall, everyone's greatest fear is loss: loss of loved ones, loss of health, one's spouse, or family members.

Women, especially single mothers, fear the effects attempting the multiple roles of parent and career person will have on their children but are afraid not to work due to economic pressures. Women today have a greater fear of random violence such as rape, robbery, car-jacking, and other crimes.

As the world grows more uncertain and violent, women's fears are escalating. Experts say the most common mental health problem women face today is *anxiety* and that women suffer far more fear, panic disorders, and distress than men. Jean Lush, therapist and author of *Women and Stress*, said recently that 71 percent of women think the world is *out of control*. It's a stressful time!

Women in Fast-Forward

As women, we may be going in fast-forward trying to keep up with the needs and demands of the roles we juggle and trying to press more into our twenty-four-hour days. Sometimes we can avoid our fears by keeping a frantic pace—being a supermom, wife, and church attendee. Yet underneath we may feel more distant from God and see Him as a taskmaster instead of a loving Father. Our fear of not measuring up may cause us to be performance-oriented, frustrated, and lonely. And a fear of failure causes many women to not use their God-given gifts and talents or pursue their unique interests. Stuffing our anxieties and frustrations, we become exhausted and find joy is absent.

When fears are denied and not dealt with, they can develop into physical symptoms, like a racing heart, light-headedness, lack of concentration, hyperventilation, and a sense of losing control. For some, these symptoms escalate into full-scale panic attacks.

I'm not referring to the kind of healthy fear that keeps us from walking into traffic on a highway and that motivates us to use child-proof caps on medicine or take any other wise precautions. God wants us to use common sense, discernment, and prevention to protect ourselves from real dangers. On the other hand, unhealthy fears often appear in the form of anxiety, says Keith Miller in *The Edge of Adventure.*[2] These fears spring from inner motivations that may or may not be grounded in reality, such as being afraid of failing, rejection by others, or getting sick. And these unhealthy fears are the ones we need to take a closer look at.

The High Cost of Fear

What a toll anxiety and fear take in our lives! It's the greatest barrier to our becoming all God means us to be. Moreover, fear, whether conscious or unconscious, has several devastating effects.

Fear causes confusion and faulty thinking. Our brains contain more than two billion megabytes of capacity to handle the challenges and problems of life. But when we're preoccupied with fear and worry, thoughts become tangled. Worrying actually blocks logical thinking.

Fear saps our energy. All of us have a certain supply of emotional and physical energy called "calendar energy." If we use it up being worried and anxious, we can literally run out of gas and burn out. I don't know about you, but I need all the energy I can get to deal with each day's challenges.

Fear harms relationships. Overworrying causes us to over-protect or control our children. Fear interferes with personal relationships, especially in marriage. If we are people-pleasers, always worrying about what we say, it prevents us from being honest with others. When we fear rejection, we tend to wear a mask. Fear can also keep us from making commitments to others and thus can sabotage close relationships.

Fear limits our potential. God has given each of us talents and gifts He wants us to use, but fear keeps those talents in the closet. It causes us to avoid new situations and miss taking advantage of opportunities to develop and utilize our gifts. "All of us have reservoirs of full potential," said Swiss psychiatrist Paul Tournier, "but the road that leads to those reservoirs is guarded by the dragon of fear."[3]

Fear sets us up for failure. "I was afraid that was going to happen!" said a mother of a teenage driver who had just had his first wreck. Fear creates what we fear; it has a magnetism that attracts or quickens the approach of the feared event! For example, if you are afraid of a dog biting you, you increase the possibility of that event happening. By focusing on your fear that you are going to gain weight, you are actually putting faith toward that happening and setting yourself up for weight gain.

Fear robs us of faith. Just like a seesaw, fear and faith rise and fall proportionately. When one increases, the other decreases. Second Timothy 1:7 says God has not given us a spirit of fear but of power and love and a sound (strong) mind. But when fear robs you of your faith, then power, strength, and a loving attitude go too.

Fear and worry steal our joy. If you're a visual person with an active imagination, you may turn your anxieties into "mental movies" that play constantly across the screen of your mind. If you're a talker who is more auditory in how you process life events, you may replay your mental tape recorder with negative messages and "What if's?" In either case, it's hard to be happy and worried at the same time!

Corrie ten Boom said, "Worry doesn't empty tomorrow of its sorrows. It empties today of its strength." It also steals your happiness today. Nothing drains your joy *and* your strength away faster than worry and fear. That's why the Bible tells us more than 366 times *not to fear!*

The good news is that you don't have to hold on to your fears; you can be free of them! You can trade your worry for wonder—*wonder* at what an adventure life becomes when you're not shackled by anxiety; *wonder* at the growth in your relationships when you let go of control; *wonder* as you discover and pursue the special gifting and purpose God has for your life; most of all, w*onder* at who God is and how great His power is toward us who believe! That's what this book is all about. In addition to my own story, there are real stories of women like you who not only faced their fears but overcame them. Woven into these stories are practical steps to take that help you leave your fears behind.

⊹⊱◈⊰⊹

Worry doesn't empty tomorrow of its sorrows.
It empties today of its strength.
—Corrie ten Boom

⊹⊱◈⊰⊹

1

The Lights Go On

I sought the Lord, and he answered me;
he delivered me from all my fears.
—Psalm 34:4

I sat on the brown and gold print couch in the living room of our little house on Delaware Place, not knowing what to do with myself. I usually spent the boys' naptime studying for my oral exams, but only a few weeks before, I'd lumbered across the stage, seven months pregnant, and received my Master's degree—now I'd done everything that was supposed to bring happiness. We had two precious boys and one child on the way. I had finished my degree, and my husband, Holmes, was doing well in the clothing business.

But at twenty-nine I found myself asking, like the old Peggy Lee song, "Is that all there is?" There seemed to be nothing else to shoot for. So busy in our individual pursuits, Holmes and I had become distant, and little resentments had piled up into walls between us. I was also struggling with worry about our son's asthma attacks. As long as I was working toward a goal, I could keep the darkness and loneliness at bay.

So that afternoon as the boys slept, I combed through the bookcase looking for something to read. A Jane Austen book I'd read twice in graduate school. A dusty Zane Grey mystery that must have been left over from the fifties. Nothing looked halfway interesting.

God, who meets us right where we are, had been drawing me back to Him through my love and study of literature. Throughout my twenties I had begun reading theologians and philosophers, searching for truth; and I found my way to Paul Tournier, Dietrich Bonhoeffer, and other philosophers. In graduate school I was drawn to the seventeenth-century British metaphysical poets who had a passion for Christ, and their poetry reflected this relationship with Him.

So, while seeking for something to read that day, my hand hit upon an old Phillips translation of the New Testament my husband had used in a college religion class. I picked it up and thumbed through it. Settling myself on the couch, I began to read it in the quiet.

I started with Matthew, read through Mark, then Luke. Day after day, page after page, I read just as I had so many books the last few years. While reading the fourth book, John, several weeks later I read those familiar words that happened to be the first I'd read and memorized as a six-year-old at home: "At the beginning God expressed himself. That personal expression, that word, was with God and was God, and he existed with God from the beginning. All creation took place through him, and none took place without him. In him appeared life and this life was the light of mankind. The light still shines in the darkness and the darkness has never put it out" (John 1:1–3, Phillips).

As I read those words, the lights went on! I realized it was God's Living Word and that every word of this book was true. I saw that Jesus was the Light who came into the world to bring light to our darkness and to my own darkness. I knew He was real. I knew that He was alive—not a God at a distance but *with us*, and He had a plan for my life. At the same time, I thought, *If this is all true, how should I be living?* His presence filled my heart and the room.

A few days later I was driving down a Tulsa street with my children, and a still, small voice seemed to answer one of my big questions, "Heaven and hell are real and start here—which path are you choosing? Who will you give your life to?"

And that day I answered a resounding "Yes, Lord! I'll go with You!"

Shortly after my reawakening, Holmes started reading this same New Testament and C. S. Lewis's *Mere Christianity*; and for the first time in our marriage, we began to talk to God together on a regular basis. It was like dark glasses being taken off: the grass looked a little greener and the sky bluer; our marriage relationship slowly began to improve.

Our life was not problem free, however. In fact our son's asthma got worse, I had an active three-year-old and a newborn to care for, and we moved to a new city three weeks after she was born. God had much to teach me. I had many layers of fears to face. But now I was aware I was not handling mothering, Justin's illness, the children's chicken pox or earaches, or life alone anymore, and it made all the difference. Most of all, I had taken a step toward the greatest adventure of my life.

⊷══◉═══⊷

Fear not for tomorrow; God is already there.
—Anonymous

⊷══◉═══⊷

The Adventure of a Lifetime

Day by day I read God's Word for marching orders, spent time talking to God and getting to know Him, and began to find out that Christianity is truly the Adventure of a Lifetime when we live it with faith in Him instead of in fear. We said, "God, we're giving up our agendas and plans; we'll do anything You want us to do."

God continued to work on my fears, peeling them back like an onion, layer by layer. Fear about losing someone I loved was at the top, so He said, "Let's face this one together." I find God rarely has us go *around* a situation when we can go *through* it with Him. He began to show me how He brings beauty out of the worst situations and life out of death and that nothing—even the death of someone we love very much—can separate us from His love. In fact, each adversity became a tool God used to bring me into more freedom and growth instead of more anxiety.

Learning to Be a Vessel

When my mother, who'd been both mother-love and father-love to me, was fifty-nine years old, she was diagnosed with cancer. The doctor told this vibrant grandmother of twenty that she had one to six months to live.

Mom was a very organized planner who wrote our names under the furniture she wanted us to have and divided up her jewelry "so we wouldn't squabble," she said. Close to the end, or actually the *beginning*, she was torn. She wanted to be well and keep gardening, going to church, and having her grand-kids visit her at the ranch. It was agonizingly hard to let us go, but she said to me one night, "I'll get to see Jesus face-to-face. After praying to Him all these years about all of you, now I can talk to Him about you up close."

She then asked me to write down the songs and plans for her "Glorious Homecoming" service, as she called it—"Great Is Thy Faithfulness," "Special Delivery," and the Scriptures she wanted read from Psalm 121 and Revelation 21. One of the songs she requested was a chorus from Isaiah 61 called "Beauty for Ashes." It was a little song we had sung almost daily that had sustained her in trying moments. When she'd had radiation or other treatment and was feeling low, she would say, "Sing 'Beauty for Ashes' for me." Somehow it seemed to lift her spirits.

"Be sure that song is sung at my service," Mama said, "and if no one in the choir can sing it, you and Holmes and the kids sing it. It's very important to me."

I wrote the song down on the list and said OK, thinking that surely the soloist, the choir, or the music director would be able to sing it. I rarely argued with Mom anyway, but especially not when she was planning her funeral!

Mom died two weeks later. I gave the directions to the pastor. Later that day he came back to me and said, "Everything's planned just as your mother wanted it, but no one in the choir has ever heard of that song."

"It goes, 'He gave me beauty for ashes, the oil of joy for mourning,'" I said, "just like in the verses in the Bible. Surely someone can sing that simple melody."

"No one wants to do it on short notice," he replied. "If it's sung, you'll have to do it. You seem to be the only person who knows it."

The next morning I woke up heavyhearted and exhausted from nights at the hospital. There was an empty hole in my heart, and sadness had settled there. I was neither a professional singer nor in any shape to sing at Mom's service, and I knew it. But I was not about to break my promise to her either. That morning in my quiet time I said, "Lord, I can't do this. But I don't want to let Mom down."

He directed me to Romans 12:1, which says to "present your bodies a living and holy sacrifice, acceptable to God, which is your spiritual service of worship" (NASB). God seemed to be saying, "Just present yourself to Me as a vessel, and I'll do the rest."

Later that day at Mama's service, Holmes and I and our three children stood up, banked by sprays of red roses and white carnations, and sang acapella the little chorus from Isaiah 61:

> He gave me beauty for ashes,
> the oil of joy for mourning
> the garment of praise
> for the spirit of heaviness
> that we might be trees of righteousness
> the planting of the Lord
> that He might be glorified.

I didn't *feel* like an oak of righteousness, but God gave me the strength I needed to sing the song I'd promised Mama. And He gave me a willing husband and three precious children to sing it with me. I didn't realize at the time how God would use that verse and the truth that I learned.

"Just Do It!"

I'd been keeping journals and writing poems about my children for several years. The desire to write was growing, yet all the pieces of writing were stuck in drawers and files. That year after Mom died I was reminded how brief life was and felt an urgency that I needed to get on with learning the craft of writing. I took a six-week freelance writers' course to learn some basics, continued my journaling, and wrote some articles.

The next year I taught in high school and was struck by how unmotivated and troubled the teenagers were and how their academic skills had fallen since the last time I'd been in the classroom, only a few years before. And these parents were paying tuition—this was a private Christian school! Parents seemed frustrated and puzzled about what to do about their children's poor performance in school.

While grading at my desk one afternoon during the spring semester, praying for and weeping over my students, the outline for a book for parents came to me with the title clearly in mind—*HOME-LIFE: The Key to Your Child's Success at School*. I was so excited about the idea that when the semester ended I "retired" from teaching, got a word processor with a little money left by my mother's estate, and started to "Just do it!" With my book proposal all typed and sample chapter under my arm, I went to a writer's conference in Minnesota that summer to learn how to write a nonfiction book.

Step by Step

It was a step-by-step process. God only showed me a glimpse, one step to take. I'd take it, and He would show me one more step and open a door. God always provided the light to take that next step.

About two-thirds of the way through the writing of my book, the publisher interested in the project dropped it. In the meantime I sent one chapter to a major women's magazine, and it was accepted as a feature article. Another I sent to *Focus on the Family* magazine, where they held it for a year and a half. Eventually, I met a publisher over lunch at a writer's conference who offered me a contract within a week. I finished the book while we were packing to move to Maine. Then nine months later, in September of 1988, the book was released, my article in *Focus* (which was a chapter) and an article in *Family Circle* came out—all in the same week! This not only led to my being interviewed on radio programs, but being asked to speak to parents' and teachers' groups.

At that point, God and I had a little chat. "Lord! I didn't sign up to speak. I just said I'd do this one book for parents and write some articles to help equip them to support their children's learning." You see, I was terrified of getting up in front of a group to speak—although I loved to talk one-on-one. I had avoided ever taking speech courses—much too anxiety-producing for me!

The Lord knew all the time I'd be too "Much-Afraid," like the character in Hannah Hurnard's book *Hind's Feet on High Places*, if He had shown me the whole blueprint. So He led me one step at a time. I accepted the first invitation, prepared a message, and then panicked. "Lord, help!" I cried, nervous even thinking about speaking to the group that night.

"Remember your mother's service? What did I show you to do?" His Spirit seemed to say. "Like in Romans 12:1, just offer yourself to Me as a living sacrifice, and I'll do the rest."

When I got up to speak to the parents' group of Yarmouth Intermediate School that first night, my hands were a little shaky and my mouth was dry. But as I began to talk, peace filled me, and I began to have fun sharing with these eager parents. Since that time, sharing with people through presentations and seminars, retreats and radio programs has become a source of much joy. Writing has been a tremendous amount of work—and certainly much more than the *one book* I had the initial idea for. But after all, God "is able to do immeasurably more than all we ask or imagine, according to his power that is at work within us" (Eph. 3:20).

In the process, I've met some precious people and had experiences I wouldn't trade for anything; at the same time, I've been able to work at home while raising our three teenagers. I would have missed all of it if I'd kept handling life on my own and being limited by my fears instead of entering into the Great Adventure—His plan instead of mine. God is full of surprises. Yes, the journey has its twists, turns, obstacles, and difficulties—some of them that threaten to overwhelm us—but all of them God uses for our good: to refine us, to prepare us, to grow our character, *and to help us face and overcome more of our fears!*

◆══◎══◆

> *Faith is like radar that sees through the fog—*
> *the reality of things at a distance that the human eye cannot see.*
> *—Corrie ten Boom*

◆══◎══◆

What burdens are you carrying? What are the fears and anxieties that weigh you down on a regular basis? In the pages ahead we will explore some of the common fears that women today experience and how you can break free to experience greater fulfillment, faith, and intimacy with God.

Suggestions for Trading Your Worry for Wonder

Keep a journal or notebook handy. You will need it for specific activities and "Bringing It Home" applications throughout the book. As you read each chapter, write out the suggested applications in your journal (identifying childhood fears, or "Glory Journal" entries, for example). Write your thoughts about the specific fears described in the chapter, feelings you experience as you read, or any memories of your own experiences that might surface while reading.

Get a package of three-by-five-inch cards to use in some of the chapter applications. You'll need these to make your "Peace Packet" and for recording verses.

Write a letter to God in your journal after you read each chapter.
Psalm 62:8 says, "Pour out your hearts to him, for God is our
refuge." Pouring out the contents of your heart and emotions
on paper is one of the best stress-reducers, and it helps clarify
what you are feeling, what God is saying, and how He is working in your life.

Record questions and insights that arise as you read. I encourage
you to discuss these and the questions in "Bringing It Home"
sections with a friend and perhaps to pray together as specific
fears are identified or needs arise.

*Note the "Lifesavers and Worrybusters" Scriptures at the ends of
most chapters.* God's Word is our best weapon against fear. It
will quench the darts of anxiety. The Word is our sword that
does effective battle against worry. The verses chosen relate to
the specific fears each chapter discusses, and they are excellent
for meditating on, praying about, and memorizing. As you
replace negative, fearful thoughts with God's promises and
truth, your fears will be transformed into faith and your worry
exchanged for wonder.

*If you would like to use this book for group study, read "Questions
for Discussion and Reflection" in the back of this book.* These questions are especially designed to provide opportunities for
interaction, for digging a little deeper, and for applying the
material in this book. Fears and anxiety are good issues to
tackle in a group setting, and this section of questions will
facilitate discussion and application.

2

Every Parent's Worst Nightmare: Overcoming Fears about Our Children

Prayer, even prayer for what God desires, releases power by the operation of a deep spiritual law; and to offer up what one loves may release still more.

—SHELDON VANAKEN

Dread tied my stomach in knots before I ever opened my eyes that September Sunday morning. Even in deep sleep I listened for the sound that sparked a fear in me that washed like waves through every nerve fiber in my body. It sounded like a death rattle, made more horrifying because it emanated from the chest of my six-year-old son, Justin.

His skin was pale and drawn; his chest heaved as he gasped for a breath. I looked into his blue eyes and saw a reflection of my own fears.

Scrambling out of bed, I ran for his inhaler. Asthma had become the embodiment of every fear I owned. I'd tried so hard to protect my children, giving them nutritious meals and vitamins, hovering over them like a quail with her covey. As I watched them play in the backyard or at the park, a nagging fear in the back of my mind made me overvigilant. Usually I broke up their conflicts instead of letting them work them out.

My husband, Holmes, accused me of being overprotective, and I knew I was. But how could I explain the horrible dread that welled up in me, especially when Justin was sick?

When asthma hit Justin at age four, it hadn't been a simple case of wheezing. His first attack had been full-blown *status asthmaticus*—the most deadly form—and took days in a hospital to bring his breathing back to normal.

That's what I hated most about asthma—I was powerless to control it. An attack could hit any moment, changing our plans. This chronic illness had stolen my joy and overtaken our lives. It had even curtailed our travel to the grandparents' ranch in Texas or anywhere else because we'd wind up in an emergency room due to the climate change.

Just as I always did, I consulted with the doctor on the phone, gave Justin all his medicine, and made sure he used his inhaler and rested. But this time nothing worked. Even with careful nursing, as the day grew longer, his wheezing worsened. Hollow-eyed, muscles and veins in his neck sticking out with each breath, Justin was scared stiff, and so was I.

So by 10:00 P.M. that night, we dropped our two younger children at a neighbor's and sped to the hospital emergency room in the rain. After several injections of adrenaline and IV medications didn't snap him out of the attack, the ER doctor called our pediatrician. When I saw him stride down the long, gray hall, I breathed a sigh of relief. *I just know he can get Justin's asthma attack under control. He always has before.*

"Raise the level of aminophyllin and cortisone. Give him another adrenaline injection," he ordered the ER nurses. "An asthma attack is like a ball rolling down a hill," Dr. Spencer told us. "We've got to stop it with the biggest guns available before it gets any closer to the bottom. Don't worry—you'll probably be home in a few hours." He turned on his heels and disappeared down the hall.

At 2:00 A.M. the nurse called Holmes and me out of the cubicle. "Your son is not responding as well as he should. You'll have to admit him to the hospital. If you'll just go down the hall to 'Admitting' and sign the papers, we'll get him upstairs to a room."

Dashed Hopes

My spirits fell like the rain pelting the window beside me. Swallowing a huge lump in my throat, I thought about the yellow Snoopy lunch box Justin had picked out, the new jeans and red plaid shirt already laid out on his bunk bed for the first big day. "Holmes, there's no way he'll be well enough to start school!"

"I think we have a lot more to worry about than school," he bristled. After we got our son all settled in his fifth floor room, Holmes sent me home to stay with Alison and Chris while he kept vigil at Justin's bedside. I just *knew* he'd be better in the morning.

But when I walked in at 8:00 A.M., Justin was white-faced, an oxygen tube in his nose. The muscles in his neck and chest strained as he fought for air. Every breath sounded like a rib-rattling staccato. In spite of other treatments, his condition worsened throughout the day. On his afternoon rounds, Dr. Spencer examined him again, shook his head, and took us out in the hall.

"Something inside his body has got to rally. I've done everything I know to do," he told us.

Stunned, I couldn't believe what I heard. My heart raced. The rising anxiety cracked the thin veneer of calm I'd tried so hard to maintain. The thing I feared the most was happening.

Fears from Childhood Past

Staring into space, I suddenly wasn't a thirty-two-year-old mother; I was a child, transported back to age eleven, coming out of our pink bedroom. Rubbing my eyes, I looked for the source of the noise and voices I heard in our home and heard Pastor Tom, our neighbor, say, "Girls, your father had a heart attack and passed away in the night. It's like he's gone through a door and you can't come, not for a long long time. . . ."

His voice was broken off by my and my sisters' sobs—sobs that continued through the next day and into the funeral in our church. Yellow Tyler roses covered my father's casket and filled the church. We sat in a long, somber row.

"Don't cry so much," my aunts said, leaning forward to our front-row pew and patting my shoulder. "You'll upset your mother."

Shaken Back to Reality

"Why don't you go home for a while?" Holmes's voice jarred me back to the present.

"But I can't leave now."

"You've got to nurse Alison and reassure Chris. They haven't seen you for hours. Besides, you aren't much help unless you pull yourself together. You're only making him nervous," he said.

I hated to leave, but I knew he was right. In a dazed fog, I rode the elevator down and walked out the front door of the hospital. A loud clap of thunder startled me. A slap of cold rain stung my face. I searched up and down the rows of parked cars but couldn't find our station wagon anywhere. Finally, soaked and shivering, I went back into the hospital to wait for the storm to let up. Huddling next to the door, I noticed the sign: "Chapel."

Reluctantly, I went into the empty chapel and was drawn to the large white Bible at the front, open to Psalm 42:5–6:

> Why are you downcast, O my soul?
>   Why so disturbed within me?
> Put your hope in God,
>   for I will yet praise him,
>   my Savior and my God.

Finally, in the quiet I prayed, "Lord, I've put my hope in the doctor, the medicine, Holmes, and myself to save Justin. That's why I'm in so much despair and fear. I've trusted You in some areas of my life, but I've clung to my kids, trying to keep them safe. I even dedicated them in a church service, but I never could entrust them totally to Your care. I'm like the disciples who in the midst of a fierce storm cried out to Jesus, 'Master, Master, we are perishing!'"

And a quiet inner voice spoke comforting words to me (as He had to the disciples), "Cheri, where is your faith? Peace, be still."

Lightning caused the chapel lights to flicker off and on, and thunder boomed outside, turning my thoughts again to God.

The Creator of the whole universe—in complete command of the thunderstorm outside, yet I can't trust Him with my son's life. In not releasing him to God's care, I'm thwarting the very power that could help him.

"Hope in Me," I felt Him say. "Trust his life to Me totally."

I bowed my head and this time said aloud, "Father, forgive me for not trusting him to Your care sooner. I forgot that he was Your child first and that You made him. I give him to You, whatever happens."

As I walked outside, something warm began to melt away that icy fear that had gripped me. The torrent of rain had turned to a drizzle. After searching several rows in the parking lot, I found our car.

I drove up the hill to get on the expressway. When I slowed at the "Yield" sign, I looked up and was struck by a tiny sliver of bright sunshine that broke through the angry, black clouds. At that moment, a huge weight lifted inside me, and a feeling of peace unlike any I'd ever experienced swept through me. Justin was safe and cared for. I knew it, and knew I could trust God.

I spent a happy, unhurried hour at home with Chris and Alison in our favorite yellow rocking chair munching cheese and crackers and reading Richard Scarry books to them.

An hour and a half later I returned to the hospital and walked into our son's room. He was sitting up in bed, coloring a picture and chatting with his grandparents, who had just arrived from East Texas. A smile lit up his rosy face as he asked, "Mom, when can I go home and see Chris and Alison and the puppy?"

Although Justin still battled asthma in the years to come, his treatment never required hospitalization again. When I packed his Snoopy lunch box on his first day of school, I sent him off with a deep sense of peace. I wouldn't be there to protect him, but I knew the One who would.

⟡

Through prayer we can open a window to God's love.

⟡

Bringing It Home

The fear of losing a child and worries about our kids' health are absolutely gripping. My heart goes out to those who have lost a child. There is no greater heartache. I know, since we lost a baby shortly after delivery. That's why I know that God doesn't always choose to answer our prayers in the way we expect but that He does help us carry our burdens.

How to Release Your Children to God

Over the years, I've spoken to hundreds of women about those fears and heartaches we have concerning our children. With their help and insight, I've learned several ways to move toward the goal of releasing this fear *and* our kids to God. Here are a few:

Mirror the truth. An Oregon woman says she struggled for years with worry about her children until she put a sign on her bathroom mirror: "Your kids are not yours. God owns them. Quit stealing!"

Review God's past goodness. One of the best ways to deal with fear is to reflect on how faithful God has been in our lives in the past.

"I'd never been a fearful person or felt vulnerable until I had children," says Deena, a mother of three. But that changed when her infant daughter Caitlin's lungs burst due to pulmonary hypertension, and she had to be airlifted to a Houston hospital in critical condition.

At that point, Deena realized how little control she had and was able to entrust her baby's medical problems to God's care.

But when she got Caitlin home after many weeks in the hospital, this young mother found herself protective and clingy.

When fear and worry gripped her, Deena made a habit of sitting down and jotting on paper all God's past goodness in their lives. "Doing this reminds me *who my children are, who God is,* and *what He's done,*" she says.

"I remind myself they're God's children, and I'm more a caretaker for them than an owner—there's a big difference! He's *their* Heavenly Father, the one who created them and promises He'll work everything in their lives for a pattern of good. And then I think of the many answered prayers, how Caitlin recovered, of the blessings that came out of difficult times."

As Deena continues listing God's goodness in this way, it's as if He loosens her grip, finger by finger, on the situation *and* the fear. As she says, "Sometimes I have as tight a grip on fear as it does on me!" Then she's freer to open her hands and heart, lay her children and their problems before God, and experience His comforting presence.

Make a Peace Packet. When Cathy's daughter Susan was going blind, she agonized over what was happening. Susan had to drop out of college, her boyfriend broke up with her, and friends seemed to disappear. The family had prayed, trusting God with the situation. But as Susan's blindness progressed rapidly that summer, Cathy found herself awakening each morning with tears running down her face. Her heart was heavy, and true peace seemed far away.

One morning when Cathy read Isaiah 26:3 (TLB), "He will keep in perfect peace all those who trust in him, whose thoughts turn often to the Lord," she had an idea: to take index cards and write down this and other verses to carry with her everywhere she went to focus her mind on throughout the day. She found her thoughts were gradually transformed from worry and sadness to a confident sense of peace. Thus she called her Ziploc bag filled with Scriptures her "Peace Packet." She was able to release her daughter to God again and rejoice in how He was working. Cathy also found she had more encouragement and a Peace Packet to give her daughter.

"The purpose of the Peace Packet is to remind us that we have a fantastic God who will be faithful to fulfill His promises," she says. The Peace Packet has not only been a source of strength to Cathy and her family but has also encouraged many women in difficult situations to trust God.

Here are suggestions for making and using your own Peace Packet:

- On a three-by-five-inch card, write out the verse that has encouraged you or speaks to your situation.

- Repeat the promise in your own words, telling God you are depending on Him. Pray out loud, believing God will do what He says! For example, "God, You said You would lift the fallen and those bent beneath their loads, that You are close to all who call on You sincerely (see Ps. 145:14–21). Now I trust You to do this in my life."

- Put the cards in a small, Ziploc bag to carry with you wherever you go.

- Pray through the verses in the morning and throughout the day (lunch, dinner, bedtime, etc.). Whenever you have a few minutes, get out a card and pray the verse.

- Add to the promises and verses in your Peace Packet as you discover them. Ask God each day to show you a new promise. Note the verses at the end of each chapter called "Lifesavers and Worrybusters."

- Share your verse with someone today. Say, "God, I want to be an encourager. Lead me to someone who needs to hear this verse or promise." When you give the verse away by sharing it with others, it truly becomes your own.

- Release your expectations. Sometimes we fear that our child won't fulfill his potential or do all the wonderful things we hoped for him. Mothers of teens and young adults who act like prodigals often struggle with particular worries.

• "I've had to release all my expectations and visions of how Ryan was going to behave during his teenage years," said his mother, Marianne. Because of losing her four-year-old daughter and husband in a tragic car wreck several years before, she had pinned all hopes on her only son and God's purpose for her future.

"Finding the right girlfriend, going on mission trips, having friends and the youth group over to our house—I had to let all those expectations go," Marianne says. She found that if she hung on to those expectations, she became disappointed and anxious. But when Marianne released her dreams and expectations for her teenage son, she recovered a sense of humor and began enjoying him again. She never stopped praying for him, but she trusted in God's timing to turn his life around instead of trying to make it happen on her schedule.

Accept God's plan when it's different from yours. Pam had been able to care for her daughter Jan since Jan was diagnosed with severe cerebral palsy as a baby. But when Jan was sixteen, they had to place her in the Children's Center, a special needs long-term care facility in their city.

"I had prayed to be allowed to take care of Jan as long as she lived. I never wanted to put her in a residential home," says Pam. But because of Jan's medical needs and because of her growing size, Pam could no longer care for her at home.

"God knows my heart and my limits. He made provision for her to be cared for in a better way than I can give." For Pam, accepting that provision is part of releasing her daughter.

Two stories in the Bible have reminded her that what is really important is to trust God to watch over Jan at the center and to remember that His plan is better than hers: Abraham's experience of laying his son on the altar by faith and Moses' mother placing him in a basket on the Nile River.

Fear of her daughter's suffering, fear of not being there for her if something happened, fear of the unknown—the only way Pam isn't overwhelmed by these possibilities is to keep her eyes on God's promises and, as she puts it, "When I can't trace God's hand, I can trust His heart."

Besides visiting Jan daily at the center, Pam has found tremendous ways to help the other parents of handicapped children there and has begun to work part-time for her church. God continues to widen her ministry and increase her joy as she trusts Him one day at a time.

Keeping Your Focus

As mothers, we have a desire to protect and care for our children that seems to come with the job description. But sometimes that caring can turn to clinging. A crisis occurs. Your child is hospitalized. The television news flashes a picture of a child kidnapped in your state. You become preoccupied with what might happen or paralyzed by a situation that seems out of your control. You check every hour during the night to see if your baby is still breathing. You don't trust anyone to baby-sit her.

When these kinds of fears plague you:

Call a friend to pray with you. Friendship divides burdens and multiplies hope. Share your concerns.

Meditate on Scripture to help keep your focus on the truth instead of the "What if's." God's promises remind you how much He cares for you and your children. Pick one verse each week to memorize and add to your "Peace Packet." See the "Lifesavers and Worrybusters" at the end of the chapter for starter verses.

Let go of your plans and expectations for each of your children and be open to what God has planned. Remember Ephesians 3:20 says He does more than you could ever ask or think.

Pray for your children daily. Praying for them helps you put them in God's hands, not only in a crisis but in everyday situations and problems as well. After all, that's the safest place for them to be! Personalize the "Lifesavers" Scriptures, putting your child's name in the verse as you pray.

Lifesavers and Worrybusters

I have loved you with an everlasting love; therefore with loving-kindness have I drawn you and have continued My faithfulness to you. (Jer. 31:3, AMP)

For God has not given us a spirit of fear, but of power and of love and of a sound mind. (2 Tim. 1:7)

Peace I leave with you; My [own] peace I now give and bequeath to you. Not as the world gives, do I give to you. Do not let your heart be troubled, neither let it be afraid—stop allowing yourselves to be agitated and disturbed; and do not permit yourselves to be fearful and intimidated and cowardly and unsettled. (John 14:27, AMP)

Do not fear, for I am with you;
Do not anxiously look about you, for I am your God.
I will strengthen you, surely I will help you,
Surely I will uphold you with My righteous right hand.
(Isa. 41:10, NASB)

Cast your burden on the LORD [releasing the weight of it] and He will sustain you: He will never allow the [consistently] righteous to be moved—made to slip, fall or fail.
(Ps. 55:22, AMP)

All your children shall be taught by the LORD, and great shall be the peace of your children. (Isa. 54:13, NKJV)

Pour out your heart like water
Before the presence of the Lord;
Lift up your hands to Him
For the life of your little ones. (Lam. 2:19, NASB)

"For this [child] I prayed, and the LORD has given me my petition which I asked of Him. So I have also dedicated him to the LORD; as long as he lives he is dedicated to the LORD. "
(1 Sam. 1:27–28, NASB)

Lord, when doubts fill my mind, when my heart is in turmoil, quiet me and give me renewed hope and cheer. (Ps. 94:19, TLB)

[God] gives power to the tired and worn out, and strength to the weak. (Isa. 40:29, TLB)

Trust in the LORD with all your heart and lean not on your own understanding; in all your ways acknowledge him, and he will make your paths straight. (Prov. 3:5–6)

3

No Money in the Bank: Overcoming Fears of Financial Insecurity

Look around you and be distressed,
Look within you and be depressed,
Look to Jesus and be at rest.
—ANONYMOUS

As she rode up the North Carolina highway, Peggy felt like a fifty-pound weight was on her shoulders. Her friend, Cynthia, sang along with a Christmas tape as she drove the car, but Peggy was preoccupied with the turmoil in her own thoughts. Just then a car passed them, loaded with laughing kids and brightly wrapped packages crammed against the back window.

It's getting so close to Christmas, Peggy thought, *but there's no sign of Christmas money at our house this year. I don't know how I'm going to pay our rent, let alone buy the children any gifts. If we could just skip the holidays. . . .*

The car veered toward the craggy, sharp rocks that jutted out on the right side of the highway. Peggy braced the dashboard. Her whole body tensed up.

"Relax," Cynthia said. "I've driven this road a hundred times. Are you always this nervous in the car?"

"No, not until our car wreck last summer," she answered, staring out the window.

It all came rushing back to Peggy as the scene flashed on the movie screen of her mind—*the curve, the motorcycle racing around the bend, heading directly toward their car—then swerving to try to miss it. In slow-motion horror, the out-of-control motorcycle flew head-on into them, burst into flames, and slid under the van. She was thrown into the dashboard, seatbelt broken. Stunned from the impact of the crash, she staggered out of the car and watched helplessly as it burned—knowing insurance wouldn't be enough to replace it.*

That car wreck had become a symbol of every out-of-control thing in Peggy's life since their move—losing her job, the piled-up medical bills, the savings account withered to nothing. She lived in a constant state of fear about not being able to pay the rent or electric bill.

The situation Peggy faced was anxiety-producing, exaggerated by the holiday season. But financial fears affect everyone in every walk of life: the farm couple who fear they'll lose the ranch that has been in the family for three generations; the small businessman unable to make payroll; the single woman who's been told her house will be repossessed if she can't make the payment.

If you've experienced anxiety about finances, you're not alone. In fact, recent studies show that women suffer even more anxiety and distress than men. A woman alone raising children has particular stresses related to finances. Many women fear that they cannot make it financially on their own if their spouse's business fails. They have a hard time believing that God really cares for them.

Dealing with Financial Fears

What can you do when your finances look like they're falling apart; when you've worked hard, paid bills, and tried to save, but the rug gets pulled out from under you?

Turn Your Fear into a Prayer

When Peggy shared with her friend what was really behind her anxiety, they were able to pray together. Fear is much like an avalanche. Once the rocks or anxious thoughts start rolling, nothing will stop them—except prayer. By talking to her

friend about her worries, Peggy received encouragement and
support. As she turned each fearful thought into a prayer, her
own perspective changed.

-–≡◉≡–-

Worry is like a rocking chair.
It gives you something to do,
but it won't get you anywhere.
—Anonymous

-–≡◉≡–-

Although things didn't turn around overnight, a few days
later Peggy decided to call the International Student Office of
a local university to ask if a student who would otherwise be
alone for the holidays might like to join their family. By sharing Christmas with a girl who was ten thousand miles from
home and had never sung a carol or heard the Christmas
story, it became one of their most meaningful holidays.

A gift shop placed an order for the miniature wreath ornaments Peggy made, providing money for a gift for each person—and a turkey dinner.

Prayer moves God in on the scene and makes us stop looking at how bad the situation is and instead remember how
powerful He is.

Go to the Word of God for Strength

Single moms have even greater financial pressures and
often no one to share them with. When Susan's husband left
her and her two young girls, she had no extended family
around to help or offer assistance in any way. "While some
single parents have parents, aunts, or sisters to give them support, I had no one," says Susan.

She was a new Christian, having accepted Christ shortly
after the divorce. One night about a year later she became
overwhelmed by grief and guilt feelings about their failed
marriage. Added to that load, intense financial and personal
pressures had piled up and burdened her to the breaking

point. "It was like the weight of the world was on my shoulders," she says.

Numb from the emotional stress of twelve-hour workdays and trying to handle the demands of single parenting with little left to give her girls at night, she didn't know if she had the strength to go on. She called a local hospital in desperation: "I feel like I'm having a nervous breakdown. Can I come in during the middle of the night if I can't make it through alone?" she asked. Just knowing she could go there helped settle her down a little.

Instead of going to the hospital, however, Susan opened her Bible to Isaiah 61 and read that the Lord was sent to heal the brokenhearted, that He could turn her mourning into joy and give her a thankful attitude for her heavy, burdened spirit. As she read the words of that chapter, it was like healing salve over her heart. She realized the strength that was available for her in Christ. She remembered how God had been with her all along, even when she wasn't consciously aware of His presence. "He was right with me—He was my husband when there was no one else." That gave Susan the confidence that God would be with her in all the challenges she faced.

Susan's motto is: "When you come to the point where He's all you have, you realize He's all you need." She found God was enough!

Through His guidance, she left a position in commercial real estate that took her away from her daughters until after dark every night. She started a house cleaning business that actually provided her more income and the flexibility to be there when her girls got home from school. The five-bedroom house they lived in needed to be sold but was badly in need of repair. Houses in their area were sitting for one to two years and selling for $10,000 off the asking price, so the house needed to be in top condition.

By her own efforts and some help from her assistant in the cleaning business, Susan took off two layers of shingles and put a new roof on, laid a new linoleum floor in the kitchen, and painted the whole house inside and out. With those improvements, the house sold for only $3,000 less than the asking price, which enabled her to buy a nice house they could afford. "God was a part of all that; He was right with me in a protective, strengthening way," Susan says.

If Susan had used up her energy with worry and emotional distress, there was no way she could have accomplished what she did. Maybe you've heard of the "3 Ds" needed for success—Desire, Discipline, and Determination. For Susan, it was a fourth D that provided the extra adrenaline to press on: Desperation! Most of all, Susan says what really turned her around, giving her the energy to persevere, was God's Word.

Review Who God Is

"Everything I know is being shaken," said Carol, a mother of three. When her husband's partnership dissolved and his health deteriorated, income plummeted, and it looked like they would have to put their house on the market. Any sense of security Carol had suddenly vaporized.

"I was frightened by the financial situation, worried about my husband, and just survived day to day in a fog," she said. By reviewing Scriptures she'd learned about God's nature and by reading them aloud daily, she discovered three truths to cling to that have turned her panic to peace: God is faithful; God is good; God loves me.

Carol also began keeping a "Glory Journal." Looking for the good things that happened each day, she listed them in a notebook: the gorgeous colors of fall leaves that blew in her yard, the progress her son made in math class, the loving care of a friend who brought her family a casserole. The Glory Journal kept her focus on the positive and helped her avoid sliding into an abyss of negativity and discouragement.

Being Expectant

How could Denise, a mother of five children, cope when their family business abruptly halted? Their fifteen-year-old business provided stage technicians, lighting, and labor for concerts in the city's main entertainment arena. Winters had always been a time of struggle for them because it's the slow season for concerts. But at 5:30 on a December Friday evening, they found out their entire contract for the year was canceled. Grocery money to feed their family of seven dwindled rapidly. Rent was due in a few days, and there was not enough money in their checking account to cover it. What kept Denise from dissolving in fear and despair?

"I've learned that the God who led the Israelites through the Red Sea is the same God who will provide for us," Denise said. "He hasn't changed just because we've lost our job."

She survived and thrived by exchanging *worry* for *wonder*: "Like walking through a museum, we're walking through life. We don't know what life is going to bring us just as we don't know what's around the corner in a museum. Instead of worrying, I've learned to be expectant and wonder, 'What's God going to do next?'"

Denise gets up each morning with a sense of anticipation and gratefulness because she knows God has a plan; He's cared for them in past lean times. Like the day a bread truck stopped in front of their house, and the bread man asked, "Could you use some bread? I've got a lot left over today, and I've finished my route. Take whatever you want." Or the friend who called and needed homeschool books, and Denise was able to sell used ones to her that day. The neighbor down the road prayed for their family and then called saying they had an extra $250 in their savings account they wanted to give them.

Learning to wonder instead of worry has not been without difficulty. Shortly after losing their yearly contract, they had to move out of their house because they couldn't afford the rent. However, they were able to find a large trailer home that actually met their family needs better. Denise found part-time work cleaning houses with a friend, and her husband found a temporary job.

"The joy and excitement in our hearts is something only God can give," says Denise. "A house, car, or job couldn't give us that kind of joy, and they won't remain. But God is going to be there no matter what."

Embrace Reality and Lean on God

"One of the pitfalls of being single is thinking that some man is going to arrive, take care of me, and rescue me from all my financial burdens," says Lynn. "If you sink into that fantasy, it's easy to fall deeper and deeper in debt," she adds. Instead, Lynn has found when she embraced the fact that for the rest of her life she was responsible but depended on God as her source, the financial area became manageable.

"I've found that no matter what happens or how bad things are, if I'm faithful to tithe, I have peace," she adds. "I've never been failed or forsaken, and I've even paid for everything my whole life, including graduate school." When Lynn was in graduate school, however, money was tight. She had an old model car, and whenever tuition was due, someone would always hit her car. It never was her fault—like the time the car was sitting on the street and a tow truck came along and bam! "The car became more and more battle-worn because I'd use the repair money on tuition instead of at the body shop, but the fees always got paid on time!"

People have sent her money anonymously; special projects have come up for earning extra income—maybe in the eleventh hour, but needs were always provided for. She's also careful to keep herself on a budget, especially for food. "It's easy as a single who doesn't like to cook for one to go out to eat too much and run up a credit card bill."

Keep the Faith and Face the Worst

When Cynthia's husband, Dave, lost his job, they purposed to keep their commitment to not incur any more debt—even to replace their old car or put their children through college. For her, the "fight of faith" was to keep believing and following what God said they were to do with their money (giving, avoiding borrowing) instead of doing things their way.

What helped Cynthia the most when she began to worry was to think things through, "What is the worst that can happen?" Then she asked herself, "Is God able?"

She decided that even if they lose their house and eat bread and water for a while, the peace God gives when they believe His promises and manage money His way is worth more than *things*, than a big car or vacation. That peace comes not by having everything they want, but by living simply and following biblical principles of finance. We can never command God to do what we want, but if we're managing money His way, then when crisis comes, we have a strong foundation—things don't get chaotic.

In facing her fears this way, Cynthia finds herself energized to wait on God, to do her part, and to see how He guides and what He does. And they haven't missed any meals—she's the best cook I know! As Pamela Reeve says, "Faith is . . . confidence in God when money is running out, not rolling in."[1]

--==◎==--

It seems to be God's plan to allow all sorts of things to happen that
would naturally cause fear, but to forestall them
by the assurance of His presence.
—Amy Carmichael

--==◎==--

You Can't Outgive God

Steve, a maintenance engineer with USAir, was bumped out of his job in North Carolina and had to go to Philadelphia for a new temporary assignment. The problem was he had to leave his family behind in North Carolina. He was also having a hard time finding an affordable room to rent.

Soon after his departure, his wife, Rita, had to have major back surgery followed by months of slow rehabilitation. One day shortly after her return home, their church's intern pastor called to check on her. He found that although she was too weak to pick up a coffee cup, she was much more worried about her husband not having a place to stay and the hotel bills piling up than she was about herself.

The young pastor placed a call to an intern from Philadelphia who promptly called his parents and asked them to take Steve in. They invited Steve home that very night. Not only did he stay there for months, but they built a real friendship.

Steve did all of their maintenance on appliances, mowing, and other repairs. At the same time, their home church met many of Rita and the children's needs—transporting the kids to and from school and church and providing meals during their dad's absence. When Steve returned, he kept the intern's car running and in good shape as a gift.

"I've learned you can't outgive God," says Rita. When they were first married and things were so tight, they didn't have a dollar to give. However, they wanted to tithe and began to give even when they didn't have money. They gave their time by teaching Sunday School and working with youth, served people on a practical level, and gave financially, knowing God would honor it no matter how much or little they gave. "He knows our hearts," says Rita.

She has found that God meets their needs regardless of whether or not she doubts. "I've questioned Him at times and asked, 'Why are You putting us through this?' and He's repeatedly shown Himself faithful through every difficult circumstance." He's shown her that even when she doesn't *feel* trusting, He'll hold her up and provide for her.

Ask and Keep on Asking

When Janice's husband's law firm underwent bankruptcy, they faced many financial consequences. Not being able to buy a car to replace their old ones that had more than 200,000 miles on them was only one problem. Her parents were both chronically ill in a neighboring state, and she had to make recurrent trips to help them. Breakdown after breakdown occurred. So a more reliable car became not a want, but a real need. Yet she and her husband couldn't even take out a loan to get a used car.

In her daily prayer, Janice began to ask God for a car—not generally "Help us with finances," but specifically: "Please, Lord, provide a car for our family." She was not led to just ask once but to keep on asking, seeking, and knocking, day after day. As she continued to ask, her sense of God's ability to provide for their needs grew. Months went by, and she began to experience and express thankfulness to God that He *was* going to provide some kind of vehicle—a newer used car, one loaned by a friend—whatever was best in His timing.

While taking her girls to swim at a local water park that summer, Janice filled out a ticket for a car giveaway and threw it in with the thousands of other tickets that had accumulated in the huge box over the season.

Then one hot August day two months later she got a call—her ticket had been drawn as a finalist. "A finalist for what?" she asked, having forgotten about the entry she filled out. She was invited to Frontier City for the big drawing but was reminded that out of one million people who had registered for the free car and out of one hundred finalists, only one would win.

A week later, Janice stood with the ninety-nine other nervous, excited finalists and their families as each person came up to draw a key out of a basket and try it in the door of the brand-new red car on stage. The woman next to her rubbed her good-luck rock. The man beside her chanted positive affirmations.

When it was Janice's turn, she walked over like all the other finalists and stuck her hand in the basket. Out came a key that looked identical to those that hadn't worked. But when she inserted her key, the car door opened—it was hers!

Although the answer to her prayer was a dramatic one, the principle remains: "Ask and it will be given to you; seek and you will find; knock and the door will be opened to you" (Matt. 7:7). Perhaps not on our timetable, or not exactly what we expected, but God is faithful when we ask. And sometimes, as in Janice's case, He does "immeasurably more than all we ask or imagine"!

Bringing It Home

Perhaps you've heard some of these ideas before, but you don't know how to apply the truths. Here are five practical ways to put them into practice when worry about finances grips your heart.

1. Make a Financial Peace Packet to help you face chal-
   lenging times (see chap. 1). Take verses such as the
   "Lifesavers and Worrybusters" at the end of this chapter that specifically apply to God's provision. Write each
   verse on a three-by-five-inch card and keep them in a
   Ziploc bag to carry in your purse. As you review these
   daily, say the promise in your own words, telling God
   you are depending on Him. Add promises and verses
   from your own Bible reading that build your confidence
   in Him and His ability to provide.

2. When you are tempted to speak anxiously about your
   situation, exchange your fearful thought for the truth,
   what God says in His Word. Personalize the promises of
   Scripture, and fear will flee. For example, instead of saying, "We'll never have enough; things are just getting
   worse," affirm: "We have everything we need to live a
   life that pleases God. It was all given to us by God's own
   power when we learned that He had invited us to share
   in His wonderful goodness" (see 2 Pet. 1:3). Apply the
   "Lifesavers" on the following pages to this principle.

3. Don't put things off—that causes more anxiety. Go
   about the business that God has given you to do; for
   most of us, that's a full plate! If debts are piling up
   because income is low, don't run from creditors; run
   toward them. Seek financial counseling from a reliable
   accountant or with Christian Financial Counseling
   (1-800-722-1976), a ministry with consultants all over
   the country. Turn your attention to the responsibilities
   right before you and do them as service to God. If
   you're not sure, ask God, "What's my part—what am I
   supposed to do?"

"When I focus on the task at hand today," says Linda,
owner of a Christian bookstore that experienced lean times, "I
get so full of being God's vehicle and serving Him, I don't
have time to worry about what is going to happen."

For Linda, that's helping customers and asking herself, *What does He want me to pray*, or *How can I help this person?* It's taking care of daily business without fretting over every detail or trying to figure out how the situation will turn out. It's letting *God be in charge* (He is anyway!) and doing her part.

4. Write in your journal all the ways God has provided in the past. Include little and big blessings He has given. As you list each blessing, you'll sense gratitude and trust growing.

5. Write down your specific fears and anxieties about finances, giving them to God one by one. Pray with a friend or spouse about the heavy burdens, and be specific about your needs. If anxious thoughts about your financial or other problems resurface (which they often do!), give them back to God right then. Release them as many times as necessary until your mind is free from fretting and worrying about them.

You and I may give our problem to God, but moments or hours later, we take it back—and start handling it ourselves. If you find you've reclaimed your "broken bike," give it back to God—and leave it there!

Lifesavers and Worrybusters

Give, and it will be given to you. A good measure, pressed down, shaken together and running over, will be poured into your lap. For with the measure you use, it will be measured to you. (Luke 6:38)

So do not worry, saying, "What shall we eat?" or "What shall we drink?" or "What shall we wear?" For the pagans run after all these things, and your heavenly Father knows that you need them. But seek first his kingdom and his righteousness, and all these things will be given to you as well. Therefore do not worry about tomorrow, for tomorrow will worry about itself. Each day has enough trouble of its own. (Matt. 6:25–34)

I was young and now I am old, yet I have never seen the righteous forsaken or their children begging bread. (Ps. 37:25)

The young lions do lack, and suffer hunger; but they who seek the LORD shall not be in want of any good thing. (Ps. 34:10, NASB)

And my God will meet all your needs according to his glorious riches in Christ Jesus. (Phil. 4:19)

I am the LORD All-Powerful, and I challenge you to put me to the test. Bring the entire ten percent [tithe] into the storehouse, so there will be food in my house. Then I will open the windows of heaven and flood you with blessing after blessing. I will also stop locusts from destroying your crops and keeping your vineyards from producing. Everyone of every nation will talk about how I have blessed you and about your wonderful land. I, the LORD All-Powerful, have spoken! (Mal. 3:10–12, *The Promise*)

You, LORD, are my shepherd. I will never be in need. (Ps. 23:1, *The Promise*)

Remember this: Whoever sows sparingly will also reap sparingly, and whoever sows generously will also reap generously. Each man should give what he has decided in his heart to give, not reluctantly or under compulsion, for God loves a cheerful giver. And God is able to make all grace abound to you, so that in all things at all times, having all that you need, you will abound in every good work. (2 Cor. 9:6–8)

Every good and perfect gift comes down from the Father who created all the lights in the heavens. (James 1:17, *The Promise*)

God cares for you, so turn all your worries over to him.
(1 Pet. 5:7, *The Promise*)

Now to him who is able to do immeasurably more than all we ask or imagine, according to his power that is at work within us, to him be glory in the church and in Christ Jesus throughout all generations, for ever and ever! (Eph. 3:20–21)

4

Knowing God in the Snowstorm: How Fear Harms Our Relationships

It is the law of the spiritual life that every act of trust
makes the next act less difficult, until at length,
if these acts are persisted in, trusting becomes,
like breathing, the natural unconscious
action of the redeemed soul.
—Hannah Whitall Smith

When you can't trust God, it's very hard to trust anyone else, especially your husband. And that lack of trust can damage relationships. I found this out by personal experience. In fact, my anxiety threatened to ruin our first Christmas together and many other car trips.

Holmes and I were on our way back from Wellington, Kansas, to Dallas for a New Year's Eve celebration of my mother's birthday. It was December 1969, and we had only been married one month. Little did Holmes know the basket case of nerves he would have sitting beside him in the car!

Since almost everyone in my family had a touch of "car phobia," I thought it normal the way my big sister threw her arms on the dashboard when she thought I was stopping too close to the car in front or how we were all such experts at backseat driving. After all, the whole family had been on the fateful trip to Ruidosa, New Mexico, when my sister Georgia fell asleep on the car door and went flying out of the car on the highway. Mama, with me in her arms, became hysterical and ran back to get her. Papa, normally reserved, was shaken as he scooped my bloody and unconscious sister up in his arms. He declared that we'd never take another family trip—and we didn't as long as he lived. Georgia survived with only abrasions from head to foot, but car phobia was the long-term effect for the rest us.

Holmes and I drove away from his grandparents' house, waving, smiling, and excited about getting back to Dallas and our little duplex in Waco. It was our first New Year's Eve as a couple. A few snowflakes were beginning to fall, and I thought it was so pretty! Having grown up in Dallas, where we saw snow only once in about every five years, I loved the way the Kansas countryside looked as we drove by the wheat fields now growing whiter and whiter. However, the more it snowed and the slicker the highway got, the more scared I became.

Holmes felt confident about driving us back to Texas safely; he'd had lots of experience driving on snow and ice while growing up in northern Oklahoma. Besides, to him this was a great adventure, and he loved adventures! However, I was petrified when we began sliding a little on the increasingly slick roads. Miss White-Knuckle-Door-Handle-Hugger clung to it as if somehow the door handle could save me. Daylight was waning, and in the dark the icy sheet we were driving on looked even more dangerous.

"Holmes, you've got to slow down!" I said, fear rising up and choking me.

"I'm only going twenty," he answered. "Relax."

Relax! I thought. This looked like a full-scale blizzard to me, and we could barely see anything ahead for the whirlwind of white snow covering the windshield. There was no way I could relax. My foot "braked" to slow us down, but that didn't work. I was so scared I could barely speak.

Holmes continued driving calmly and steadily. As we drove through several small towns, the snow was drifting. It was clear by the way cars were careening off the road that there was a sheet of ice underneath the snow. When we slid off to one side several times, Holmes patiently got us back in the center of the one lane that was open.

"Holmes, why don't we just stop?"

"We don't have the option of stopping, Cheri. We're between towns, and it's too cold to pull to the side of the road. We'd freeze."

"Then let's spend the night in the next little town and continue driving in the morning when the roads are better." As soon as we slid into the next town, we passed several motels, but they all had "No Vacancy" signs out. My spirits fell.

"Look! There's a sign saying travelers can stay at the high school gymnasium overnight because of the snowstorm," I said, thinking that was a great idea.

"Your family is expecting us for the birthday party, and I'm not about to sleep on a cold, hard gym floor tonight."

Sleeping on a gym floor sounded better to me than six to eight more hours of this stressful driving. And plenty of people who agreed were turning into the school ahead of us!

"There's no reason to stop," he bristled. "We're fine, and I'll get us to Dallas safely."

With each mile Holmes grew more irritated by my nervousness. I felt increasingly hurt because he didn't understand. He didn't appreciate my many suggestions. He thought he *was* driving carefully and felt criticized. Anger, fear, and hurt welled up in me, and he couldn't relate.

When we finally arrived at my parents' home in Dallas well after midnight that New Year's Eve, I was shaken and worn out from the stressful drive, and Holmes and I were barely speaking. Unfortunately, this was a scene that was repeated in different degrees and places throughout the early years of our marriage. Between the normally peace-loving, low-conflict two of us, some of our worst times were in the car.

God Intervenes

One of the wonderful things about God is that He knows we are dust but loves us anyway. He knows our needs even before we ask, and He knows what is underneath the weaknesses when we are clueless (I guess that's part of His "omniscience"). And when we let Him, God intervenes in our lives to transform our fears and heal our hurts.

As Holmes and I were growing in Christ, we had given God our marriage along with other parts of our lives. When Holmes gave God his smoking habit, the desire totally left him, and he never smoked after that day. We told God we'd go any direction He wanted, and God had opened up exciting new doors for Holmes. We knew our relationship needed His help and healing (in eight years a lot of resentment and negative patterns can build up), but since we couldn't afford counseling, we had no idea *how* God could bring about change.

In 1978 Holmes and I attended a "Restoration Weekend" conference in our city sponsored by the Presbyterian Renewal Ministries on Restoring the Family, Church, and Nation. Peter Marshall was the speaker, and we were inspired by hearing him all three nights. On Sunday there was to be a "Healing Service." We had never attended a healing service before but thought it sounded like a good idea. Since our son's asthma had been out of control for two years despite all the medication, allergy shots, and diet changes, we looked forward to the opportunity to have Justin's asthma prayed for.

So on Sunday afternoon we sat with our children at the back of the auditorium with several hundred other people. After the message, the audience was instructed to write their requests on the piece of paper provided in the bulletin and to come up front to one of the ministers to be prayed for.

Following a wise Presbyterian pastor's message on what the Bible had to say about healing, I felt he was the best person to pray for Justin. So after writing down our request—"Our son has severe asthma and chronic allergies. He's been hospitalized frequently since he was four years old. Could you pray for him?"—we hesitantly got in the pastor's line. However, his line was so long that we were steered over to Peter Marshall.

We sat down on the pew before him when it was our turn for prayer. Peter didn't know us, but he looked intently down the row at each of us and at our son. Then he looked back at me and said, "*You're* the one who really needs prayer. Come up and let me pray for you."

I was thinking, *But you don't understand. Justin needs prayer for his asthma. That's what we came for.* But I was not one to argue with the person in charge. Holmes walked up with me, and Rev. Marshall began to pray.

Somehow God gave this man who had lost his own father when he was ten years old the knowledge that losing my father when I was a child left me with a sense of being abandoned by God, resulting in a lack of trust and many fears. I didn't trust *any* man, not even my husband. Not that I told Rev. Marshall; still, he prayed with compassion for God to heal all those emotions and for me to see how faithful my heavenly Father is, how He had led me and protected me all through my life. He prayed for trust to be rebuilt between me and my husband. As he spoke to God on our behalf, a deep root of fear and distrust began to be removed.

As Peter prayed for me, my reserved husband began to weep uncontrollably, the hurt literally pouring out of him for my never trusting him to drive safely enough or handle decisions or anything else. I'd never seen Holmes cry like this in our whole marriage. Resentment and irritations were washed from both of us as the tears flowed. Peter continued praying for our marriage to be healed and for us to truly "cleave" to one another and become *one*.

On Sunday night following the Healing Service, Peter asked married couples who so desired to stand and renew their vows. In that moment when Holmes and I repeated the wedding vows, we felt that we had gotten remarried. It was a fresh, new start—for me, of trusting God in new ways and especially trusting Him working through my husband. For both of us, the weekend brought a renewal of our love for each other and healing to our marriage. Although our son was not prayed for as was *our* plan, his asthma did begin to improve after that weekend. "In quietness and confidence is your strength," says Isaiah 30:15 (TLB). With my confidence and trust renewed in

God, I handled Justin's health problems and asthma attacks with more calm and reliance on God.

And most important, my focus had shifted from the circumstances to the One who made us and sustained us. I got a new glimpse of God. I was filled with wonder at a God so awesome He was in charge of the whole universe yet so precious that He would send a man like Peter Marshall from across the country, a man whose father had died when he was a child, just as mine had. Truly he prayed and comforted with the comfort he had received from God.

Fear Hinders Relationships

Maybe your fear isn't a lack of trust in a person as I experienced but a fear of being abandoned or rejected. That kind of fear usually causes a woman to build walls around herself, and in the process she grows lonelier and lonelier. Or fear of rejection may lead her to extreme people-pleasing and being taken advantage of by friends and family. "One of my biggest fears is investing time and heart in a friendship and then seeing my female friend marry and move away," says one single woman. "It's happened over and over, and I come up empty."

Each of us develops our own strategies for coping with this built-in fear of rejection, says Bruce Larsen in *Living Beyond Our Fears*. "One obvious one is withdrawal or shyness. We seek safety in going unnoticed. We reach out to no one lest we be rebuffed. Jesus commanded the disciples to 'love one another as I have loved you' (John 15:12, RSV). Shyness utterly stifles the ability to do that and, in that sense, could be considered a sin. You retreat from any attempt to love or be loved."[1]

How to Deal with Relationship Fears

Instead, we can let our anxieties about relationships drive us to the cross. For as Larsen says, "Fear is the handle by which we lay hold of God."[2] Laying hold of God enables us to overcome our fears and receive His love for us—a love that even drives out the fear of rejection. Whether it is the fear of not having the relationships you want or fear of losing a close friend, you can learn to handle your relationship fears.

Verbally share your fear with someone else. When you confess what you're afraid of, your fear shrinks to a manageable size, and solutions begin to come into view. When you hide the fear inside your head and heart, it multiplies and isolates you from other people.

The very heart of our fear of rejection is a sense of low self-worth, reinforced by misbeliefs we hold about ourselves. Exchange every misbelief about yourself with the *truth* about who you are in Christ. Overrule what you think or feel with what is true about you according to Scripture. For example, if you think, *I am unworthy and unacceptable*, God's Word says you *are* accepted and worthy: "I am fearfully and wonderfully made; your works [including me, your handiwork] are wonderful, I know that full well" (Ps. 139:14)

When you feel, *There is nothing special about me*, remember that God says you have been chosen and set apart by Him: "It is because of him that you are in Christ Jesus, who has become for us wisdom from God—that is, our righteousness, holiness and redemption" (1 Cor. 1:30; see Eph. 1:4; Heb. 10:10,14).

When you think, *I am unwanted*, or *I don't belong to anyone*, review the truth that you have been adopted by God Himself, and you are His child (see Rom. 8:16–17; Gal. 4:5; 1 John 3:1–2). As you focus your mind on the truth, a confident sense of "Christ-consciousness" will replace your self-consciousness, and you will be freer to love others, love God, and love yourself.[3]

Combat the fear of rejection or loneliness by becoming an encourager. Like Barnabas, one of my favorite New Testament heroes, we can become an encourager of others. As Hebrews states: "Let us consider how we may spur one another on toward love and good deeds. Let us not give up meeting together, . . . but *let us encourage one another—and all the more as you see the Day approaching*" (Heb. 10:24–25, italics added).

When you set your focus on giving the gift of encouraging words, showing appreciation for others, writing notes of thanks, and delivering help, support, hope, kindness, reassurance, and faith to others on a daily basis (for that's what the word *encouragement* means!), loneliness begins to flee, and your heart, having given much, receives much.

Most of all, anchor yourself deeply in God's love by knowing Him.

Focusing on God: Antidote to Anxiety

I'm convinced that it's our puny or inadequate perspective of God that is the root of many of our fears. And I know when I let anxiety—over relationships, finances, the future, or anything else—sap my strength, it's because I've forgotten how incredible God is! The Bible says that "those who know your name will trust in you; for you, LORD, have never forsaken those who seek you" (Ps. 9:10). We have faith in God because we *know Him*. And faith is the opposite of fear.

"Faith is a redirecting of our sight, a getting out of the focus of our own vision and getting God into focus. Faith looks out instead of in and the whole life falls into line."[4]

Thus I have found that when I become anxious or fretful, one of the best antidotes is to *refocus on God* and His names. So I kneel and praise God that He is El Elyon, the Most High God; that He is Elohim, Creator of the whole universe, yet He cares about me and my family. Then I continue praising God by remembering His names, which I've written on a card in my Bible:

- He is Jehovah-*nissi*, the Lord My Banner, and His banner over me is love.

- He is Jehovah-*jireh*, the Lord Will Provide, and He sees and knows my needs and provides for them.

- He is Jehovah-*shalom*, the Lord Is Peace—and I ask Him to fill me with His peace.

- He is El Shaddai, the All-Sufficient One, who, like a mother nurturing her children, is sufficient for all our needs.

- He is Jehovah-*raah*, the Lord My Shepherd, who promises to lead and guide me and to show me what direction to go, whether I'm in the valley or on the mountaintops.

- He is Jehovah-*rapha*, the Lord Who Heals, the One who makes even bitter experiences sweet as we trust them to Him.

- He is Jehovah-*shammah*, The Lord Is There, so that I can confidently say, "The Lord is my Helper! I won't fear or be terrified because He is with me." Wherever we are, *God is with us!* This is great news and one of my favorite of His names to think about.

- I also praise God as Jehovah-*tsidkenu*, The Lord Our Righteousness. Because of Jesus, God forgives our sins and puts upon us the breastplate of His righteousness.

In reminding myself of who God is, by reviewing and thanking Him for these and other of His names and what that part of His character means to me, I can banish anxiety and experience His peace even when a storm is raging in my life.

Fearing God Instead of Circumstances

Just as we don't trust our secrets with a neighbor or associate we have just met, we don't trust God with our daily cares and anxieties when we don't know Him intimately. We only confide in our closest friends—friends we've come to trust and know through regular, ongoing times together of sharing and listening enough to know they care. Then we're confident we can trust that friend with the deepest or most painful concerns of our lives.

Whereas fear of circumstances directs us to a horizontal focus and can paralyze us, throw us into a pity party, and consume us with worry, fear of God—which means an awe and wonder at who He is—leads us to a vertical focus and propels us to worship and enjoy Him.

⊷═◉═⊷

*To adore God means we love Him with
all the powers within us. We love Him
with fear and wonder and yearning and awe.*
—A. W. Tozer

⊷═◉═⊷

An unhealthy fear of God is shrinking from Him because we think He's going to hurt us. It's avoiding turning our lives over to Him completely because we don't trust what He'll do with them. In contrast, a healthy reverence of the Lord, the Bible tells us, is clean; it prolongs life and is the beginning of wisdom (see Pss. 19:9; 111:10). The benefits of having a worshipful wonder of God are terrific!

If we know the incredible power of the One who holds the future, then we don't fear the future, even if it looks uncertain, *for He is with us* (see Ps. 23:4).

Exploring God's Character

For two years while leading a Moms in Touch prayer group for my children's school, I looked for a different attribute of God to focus on in our praise time. Week by week I searched the Scriptures for God's attributes, and I never ran out of material. In fact, I found we'll never run out of different ways to praise Him. Focusing on God's character and attributes became a real highlight of the week for me and increased my communion with Him. God longs to reveal Himself to us. As I meditated on who He is, my joy, trust, and gratefulness increased, while anxiety—about my teenagers, our finances, the tight deadlines for magazine articles, a book, and speaking engagements—decreased.

Here are four ways to focus on and learn more about the nature and character of God:

Conduct a God Search. This is not a word search, for you're looking for God. You'll need your Bible (preferably with a concordance), a dictionary, and journal or notebook. Start with *A* and go through the alphabet looking for words that describe who God is or what He is like that begin with that letter. Make a section or page for each letter of the alphabet. Then in your daily Bible reading, be alert for any description of God that begins with an *A.*

The first one I found was *able.* I looked up all the references to God's being *able* and was surprised at how many there were. For example, in Daniel 3:17, He was *able* to deliver Shadrach, Meshach, and Abednego from the fiery furnace. God was *able* to raise up descendants from Abraham although he and Sarah were past childbearing years.

Romans 4:21 tells us that "what He had promised, He was *able* also to perform" (NASB). Second Corinthians 9:8 says, "God is *able* to make all grace abound to you, so that in all things at all times, having all that you need, you will abound in every good work." Some of the best news of all is that He is *able* to keep everything that I commit or entrust to Him, and He is "*able* to do immeasurably more than all we ask or imagine, according to his power that is at work within us" (Eph. 3:20, italics added).

Write down the verses under the first letter of the alphabet. As your list grows of all the ways God is able, your faith will be strengthened, and your wonder at this mighty God we serve will expand. Next go on to *B* (Beauty, Beloved, Bridegroom), *C* for Comforter, Counselor, or Compassion, and so on through the alphabet.

Use the Psalms as a springboard. Psalms is a book of praises. Almost every psalm is filled with aspects of God's nature, His names, and His benefits to those who trust and love Him. "God is my stronghold, the God who shows me lovingkindness," says David in Psalm 59:17 (NASB). The Psalms overflow with portraits of God.

Read a psalm each day and turn it into your own prayer, your very own praise of God. Before you read, *ask God to show you a specific Scripture in the Psalms to praise Him with that day.* Look for different facets of God's nature. In Psalms we see He's a Father of tender mercies yet disciplines His children so we will be "fit for heaven." He weeps over us, sings over us, and comforts us. Many psalms express the majestic side of God, revealing Him as King. Ask Him to reveal more of His nature to you as you read the psalm for the day: "Open my mind and let me discover the wonders of your Law" (Ps. 119:18, *The Promise*).

Use music to focus on God's character. Singing can combat fear. In chains and not knowing what persecution they faced next, Paul and Silas sang praises. God intervened, and they were suddenly and miraculously released from prison. We, too, can be released from the prison of fear when we sing to Him.

⊹≡◉≡⊹

> *Music speaks what cannot be expressed*
> *Soothes the mind and gives it rest*
> *Heals the heart and makes it whole*
> *Flows from heaven to the soul.*
> *—Anonymous*

⊹≡◉≡⊹

When I am the most concerned and anxious about a person, problem, or situation, one of the best ways I've found to refocus on God Himself and get my eyes off the fear-inducing situation is to put a praise tape on, get alone, and spend time praising God in song. As I sing about this Wonderful Counselor, Mighty God, Everlasting Father, Prince of Peace, my faith in His ability to handle the situation or person expands, and the worry gradually goes away. Joy returns and peace settles in my heart as I praise God through music.

In anxiety-triggering situations, remember the times God has spoken to you, moved, and intervened in your life. In 1 Samuel 21: 1–9 David is running from Saul. Fearful and unarmed, he comes to Ahimelech, the priest in Nob, and asks if he has any weapons. Ahimelech tells David that the sword of Goliath, whom David had killed in the Valley of Elah, is there. In taking possession of Goliath's sword, David is reminded of God's intervention in the past and is encouraged and strengthened for the battle he is facing.

What Scripture has God spoken to you before? What worked when you were in a battle or storm—was it meditating on a specific Scripture? praising Him in song? praying with a friend? Think of a time God intervened in your circumstances and moved "mountains." Remember His faithfulness! As Jeremiah says in Lamentations 3:21–23: "This I recall to my mind, / Therefore I have hope. The LORD's lovingkindnesses indeed never cease, / For His compassions never fail. / They are new every morning; /Great is Thy faithfulness" (NASB).

As you go about your "God Search," using the Psalms as a springboard to praise God, your love for God will grow, your "knowing Him" will deepen, and your anxiety will dissipate. His perfect love casts out all fear.

Another Snowstorm, a Different Response

Many situations in our lives are like being in a snowstorm; we can't see exactly what's ahead, so there's uncertainty. We're not in control, and there's danger of crashing or going off the road. Such situations also tend not to be one-time events, for we may have to go through another snowstorm!

Several years after our prayer experience on Restoration Weekend, my husband and I and our three children were on our way to Denver, Colorado, to visit my brother George and his wife. Late at night, we were driving through western Oklahoma with Justin, Chris, and Alison asleep in the back seat.

Suddenly, out of nowhere a blinding white mass of snow streamed horizontally toward our windshield. We couldn't see the stripes on the two-lane road or even the side of the road for the blizzard that surrounded us.

That old fear began rising within me. I suggested Holmes slow down, pull over, and stop. My hand gripped the armrest with every ounce of energy I had, hoping for some semblance of control. At first he was prickly and then more irritated with my anxiety. So I went right to God and began to pray, "Lord, please help me with this. I know Your perfect love casts out all fear, so I pray that You would fill me to overflowing with Your perfect love so I can somehow relax. Help, Lord!"

As I continued to pray, a song with a peaceful melody began to bubble up in my consciousness. "When I am afraid, I will trust in Thee," the words played in my mind. "In God whose Word I praise; in God I have put my trust. I shall not be afraid, no, I shall not be afraid!"

Over and over I sang this tune, first in my head and then quietly aloud. As I sang, my fear got smaller and smaller. The anxiety literally shrank before me, and I grew more calm and relaxed. My faith in God's ability and in Holmes's driving also increased. My hand relaxed its grip on the armrest, my sense of humor returned, and we eventually drove out of the blizzard.

I've never forgotten the melody God gave me in those moments during the highway blizzard. The words of the song, which I found in my Bible when we got to our destination, were from Psalm 56:3–4, almost word for word. The Holy Spirit has brought those words to mind at other times when I was afraid and needed to remember who I'd put my trust in. They are just as true today. God never fails or forsakes us, and His Word never fails.

Climbing Up in Daddy's Arms

One Sunday recently just as we were singing the words, "There's no place I'd rather be in your arms of love, in your arms of love, holding me still holding me near in your arms of love,"[5] I noticed Bonnie, a little girl I teach in first grade Sunday School, going up and down the aisles looking for her dad. She had a bewildered look on her face as she passed each row, but she was persistent about looking up and down each one until she found him.

Finally she arrived at our aisle and saw her daddy a few seats down from me. She climbed around me and several others, literally leaped up in her father's arms, and rested her head on his shoulder. As the song continued, he held her small hand in his, and the biggest smile I've ever seen lit her face up. She was *home!* This picture of what we were singing struck me: God wants our hearts to come home to Him. He wants us to feel that same kind of daddy-love from Him as Bonnie did with her dad, only much more.

First John 4:18 tells us that we don't have to fear someone who loves us perfectly as God does. Or as *The Message* translation puts it, "There is no room in love for fear. Well-formed love banishes fear." Knowing His complete and total love for us delivers us from any dread or worry of what He might do to us or what life would deal us.

An End in Itself

Although I believe that knowing God intimately is the best antidote to fear, there is a much greater, more eternal reason to know God than just living a life free of fear and worry. Knowing God through trusting our life to the lordship of Jesus Christ is an end in itself. In fact, it is *the* end, as the ancient tradition of the Heidelberg Catechism states: "The chief end of man is to glorify God and to enjoy Him forever."

As A. W. Tozer said: "God is not asking you to come to Christ just to attain peace of mind or to make you a better businessman or woman. You were created to worship. God wants you to know His redemption so you will desire to worship and praise Him."[6]

What an invitation! If you don't know God through a relationship with Christ, take time to ask Him into your heart and life, to reveal Himself to you, and to fit you for heaven so you will live with Him forever!

My prayer is that whatever you go through—be it snowstorm, high winds, or big waves that seem to rock your boat and bring upheaval and difficulty your way—you'll let it drive you into the arms of your Heavenly Father, and you'll find rest in His everlasting, always-available love for *you*.

Suggested Reading

The Knowledge of the Holy, A. W. Tozer
The Creator, My Confidant, Cynthia Heald
Lord, I Want to Know You, Kay Arthur
The Attributes of God, Arthur W. Pink
Knowing God, J. I. Packer
Desiring God, John Piper
Experiencing God, Henry Blackaby and Claude King

Lifesavers and Worrybusters

We need have no fear of someone who loves us perfectly; his perfect love for us eliminates all dread of what he might do to us. If we are afraid, it is for fear of what he might do to us, and shows that we are not fully convinced that he really loves us. So you see, our love for him comes as a result of his loving us first. (1 John 4:18–19, TLB)

God is love, and anyone who lives in love is living with God and God is living in him. And as we live with Christ, our love grows more perfect and complete; so we will not be ashamed and embarrassed at the day of judgment, but can face him with confidence and joy because he loves us and we love him too. (1 John 4:16–17, TLB)

For the Lord God, the Holy One of Israel, says: Only in returning to me and waiting for me will you be saved; in quietness and confidence is your strength. (Isa. 30:15, TLB)

Those who know Your name will trust in You, for You, O LORD, have never forsaken those who seek You. (Ps. 9:10)

When I am afraid
I will put my trust in Thee.
In God, whose word I praise,
In God I have put my trust;
I shall not be afraid. (Ps. 56:3–4, NASB)

My heart is steadfast, O God, my heart is steadfast;
I will sing, yes, I will sing praises!" (Ps. 57:7, NASB)

Therefore, since we have been justified through faith, we have peace with God through our Lord Jesus Christ. (Rom. 5:1)

The LORD gives perfect peace
to those whose faith is firm.
So always trust the LORD
because he is forever our mighty rock.
(Isa. 26:3, *The Promise*)

Do not tremble and do not be afraid. . . . Is there any
God besides Me, or is there any other Rock? I know of none.
(Isa. 44:8, NASB)

5

Facing Our Fears Head-on: Overcoming a Fear of Flying

O Shepherd, you said you would make my feet like hinds' feet and set me upon mine High Places.
—HANNAH HURNARD

One of the nicest things God did for me was to put me in the sky—literally—to face my fears, traveling alone by plane to speak to people I didn't know and doing it often enough to learn to enjoy it. You see, to me, flying was like facing cruel and unusual punishment. Each time the plane took off, I was convinced it would be my last flight. Whenever I walked through the skyway to my seat I thought about how my family could divide up my small possessions and wondered who would take care of my children. My clammy hands gripped the armrest as if I could steer the plane and somehow help the pilot. Of course, that is one of the problems with flying—backseat driving is *not* permitted. My appetite plummeted with the falling sensation in my stomach upon take-off.

I was glad to find out recently that I was not alone. An estimated twenty-five million Americans are so scared they won't even board an airplane. Another thirty million are "anxious fliers," who fly because of their jobs or emergencies but are uncomfortable aloft. (That was where I fit in.)

"*I'll Never Fly Again!*"

I think I received the fear of flying as I did many of my other fears—in utero. My mother had a deep fear of flying, perhaps from growing up in an era when it was a rarity. Riding in a car could induce anxiety, but a plane ride was out of the question. "I have too many dependents," she'd say, referring to me and my five siblings. But the major event that clipped Mama's wings was a terrific offshore storm she encountered while on a plane en route from Florida to Dallas. My stepfather had talked her into a restful trip to Florida, and she finally agreed, being a lover of the beach.

Even before she stepped onto that fateful airplane, thunderstorms and lightning terrified Mama. Whenever a storm blew over their East Texas ranch, she would insist everyone—grandkids, guests, sons-in-law—join her in the musty bomb shelter below the ground.

Up there 25,000 feet in the sky with the wind whipping the plane around, the rain beating on the windows, and her stomach in her throat, Mom promised God she would never fly again if only He would get her down on the ground safely. And she kept her promise!

She kept the "promise"—until twenty years later when her desire to see her new grandson overshadowed her fear of flying. Mom was in a hospital in Las Vegas suffering from cancer that had spread to her lungs and then her brain. Her newest grandbaby, Zachary, her only son George's first child, had just been born in Dallas. Did she ever want to see that precious grandson and hold him in her arms before she died!

However, Mom's physicians would not release her from the hospital to be driven back across the hundreds of miles to Texas because they felt she would die on the way. Flying her home was the only possibility, they said, but even that risk was too great. Because of her brain swelling, they refused to approve her flight. So my determined mom, a fiercely loving and loyal grandmother, signed forms releasing the doctors of any responsibility. She was driven to the airport, wheeled in a wheelchair to a jet, and had the most glorious flight of her life into a brilliant rosy purple glow of the Texas sunset—to a great homecoming in the Dallas-Fort Worth terminal and the chance to hold her new grandson in her arms and once again see all her beloved six children, twenty-two grandchildren, and friends.

What made the difference and why was Mom able to face her fear of flying and overcome it?

What she learned in that situation made all the difference not only in her overcoming, but also in *my* facing my fear of flight—and death also.

Set Free

A week before the "glorious flight," when Mama was very ill in the hospital, a local minister had stopped by to visit her—prompted by a friend who phoned from Texas.

After the usual hospital pleasantries, the elderly pastor and Mom began to talk. She shared all the things she had hoped to do before she died: She wanted to testify to God's goodness in her favorite churches, Main Street Baptist in Grand Saline and Jupiter Road in Garland. She had planned a family gathering with all of us in attendance; she had her jewelry and little treasures to hand out to us. She hoped to see more sunrises on her beloved East Texas ranch; and most of all, she wanted to hold her new grandson.

Not that Mom feared the end of this life. She saw it as a homecoming, a graduation. But she told the pastor she *was* anxious about the timing and worried about how long she had left because she had a lot to do! This was the organized lady I described in chapter 1 who kept everything clean and in its place. It was late June, and since the doctor's warnings she feared she couldn't possibly get home to Texas.

This wise, silver-haired pastor read to Mom Psalm 139: "O Lord, you have searched me and You know me. /You know when I sit and when I rise; /You perceive my thoughts from afar. . . ."

He stopped at verse 16: "*All the days ordained for me were written in your book before one of them came to be*" (italics added).

As he read those verses, the truth of God's Word sunk in. Mom didn't have to worry about how many days she had left because they were already written in His book. You could say the words from that familiar psalm suddenly moved from her head to her heart. In fact, those words set Mom free to celebrate not only every one of the days she had left on this earth, but also to thoroughly enjoy the best flight of her lifetime.

Through seeing Mom freed from her fear of flying and her anxiety about "how many days," the truth of Psalm 139 deepened in my own life. I came to rest in a sense of God's amazing sovereignty—whether we are on the ground or in the air. So this formerly Much-Afraid-of-the-High-Places, white-knuckle flyer now truly enjoys air time with a magazine or a good book, my journal, peanuts and orange juice—whether in a small prop plane or a jumbo jet.

That's why I'm grateful for all the flying opportunities I've had in the last ten years due to speaking engagements. They have given me a chance to become "desensitized" and to practice this overcoming attitude about flying. Because when we face our fears head-on and *do* the thing we fear instead of shrinking from it, the fears usually diminish.

⊷≡◉═⊷

Do the thing you fear most
and the death of fear is certain.
—*Victor Frankl*

⊷≡◉═⊷

Confrontation and Virtual Reality

A medical care program in California has successfully used this confrontational method—with a high-tech twist—to treat patients suffering from a fear of heights (acrophobia). The principle isn't new; it's just a modern version of facing one's fears, a technique that has been effective in treating phobias since the sixties.

In order to diminish an irrational fear of snakes, for example, the therapists have the patient confront snakes—from looking at pictures and handling stuffed or toy snakes to actually touching a living although harmless reptile. By facing his fears and practicing dealing with whatever he is afraid of, the person's anxieties begin to dissolve.

In contrast, if you avoid everything you are afraid of, the fear *escalates*. Anxiety feeds on itself. Then you begin to fear the feeling of fear: "I don't want to fly because I can't stand that awful feeling of fear I get when I'm in an airplane." "I don't want to go to the mall because I'm afraid I'll have a panic attack." Fears graduate in size to the point of agoraphobia, whose sufferers are so fearful they won't leave their own houses.

The psychologist in this new program helped his patients who were afraid of heights to face and overcome their fears by using "virtual reality," a futuristic technology in which he equipped each person with a virtual reality helmet and a joystick. Then via an interactive, computer-generated environment, they were confronted with the heights—in this case, a walk across the Golden Gate Bridge—without ever leaving the safety of the doctor's office. The anxious subjects shook, teetered, and even cried as they inched across the bridge while the psychologist instructed them to focus on their breathing and muscle tension. After just one hour of virtual reality heights, the patients made significant progress in overcoming their fears of high places.

Unfortunately, due to the expense, not everyone who is afraid can take advantage of such high-tech treatment. But we have something even more effective to help overcome our fears: God's grace and "the utter extravagance of his work in us who trust him—endless energy, boundless strength!" (Eph. 1:18, *The Message*). With the surpassing greatness of His power toward us, we can face what we fear, confront it, and feel the anxiety diminish.

Thus, one of God's best methods of recovery seems to be giving us chance after chance to do the very thing we'd like to avoid. As Dale Carnegie said, the chief cause of people's fear of public speaking is simply that they are not accustomed to speaking in public.[1] Therefore, a routine part of his famous course is regular, weekly public speaking for all participants. Practice, practice, practice in the fearful situation. The result? The participants' fears diminish.

"I Want Off This Plane!"

My mother and I aren't the only women who were hesitant about a plane ride. Melanie, a cardiac care nurse, could identify with our fears.

"My first flight was to Europe with my husband, a thirteen-hour ordeal," says Melanie, who had been scared of heights since she was a child. "I didn't go to the bathroom for thirteen hours on the jumbo jet, convinced if one more person stood up, the whole plane would tip over and crash, killing us all," she says.

Crying, she begged her husband and the stewardess, "I want off this plane! I want to go down!" They pointed out the window and down at the Atlantic Ocean, "Look down there; I don't think you want off!"

Her body tense and her imagination going wild, Melanie looked below them and thought she saw sharks with their jaws opened wide saying, "Come on down!" Her fears intensified. She got little empathy from her husband. Irritated with her anxiety, he kept reminding her that it was *ridiculous* to be afraid.

The whole month of travel in Europe was tainted by her dread of getting back on that plane. And this was supposed to be a romantic trip! The return jet was much smaller, more turbulent and shaky. The bottom of the plane was like ice, which added to her already shivering condition. The hours seemed to go on forever. Finally they landed in Chicago, where she immediately hit the runway and started kissing the ground.

Two years later Melanie reluctantly agreed to go on a church trip to Israel and Greece and endured hearing her traveling companions make fun of her fear of flight the whole way. *That's it*, she thought. *I've had it with flying; I'm staying on the ground.*

But God, who hates to see us shackled by fear, had other plans. If we have set our hearts on seeking the Shepherd and knowing Him in a deeper way, He usually arranges a way not to escape but to face our fears with His grace.

Melanie reminded me of Much-Afraid in Hannah Hurnard's wonderful book, *Hinds' Feet on High Places*. This extended allegory is about how Much-Afraid escaped from her Fearing relatives and went with the Shepherd to the High Places, where "perfect love casteth out fear."[2]

Much-Afraid had served the Chief Shepherd for several years and longed to please him, but she found two things hindered her service: physical disfigurement and a lifetime pattern of fear. In fact, she was afflicted by her own anxieties as well as by those passed down through parents and relatives. Much-Afraid was a member of the "Family of Fearings"—relatives she couldn't seem to escape from and who always tormented and terrified her.

At her request to leave the Valley of Humiliation and the almost-certain marriage planned between her and cousin Craven Fear, the Shepherd begins taking her on a journey to the High Places where perfect love reigns. On the way he leads her to dangerous precipices and steep mountains.

"I never dreamed you would do anything like this!" Much-Afraid says on one of the steep ledges. "Lead me to an impassable precipice up which nothing can go but deer and goats, when I'm no more like a deer or a goat than is a jellyfish . . . it's too preposterously absurd!"

The Shepherd laughed too. "I love doing preposterous things," he replied. "Why, I don't know anything more exhilarating and delightful than turning weakness into strength, and fear into faith, and that which has been marred into perfection. If there is one thing more than another which I would enjoy doing at this moment it is turning a jellyfish into a mountain goat."[3]

From Fearful Jellyfish to Graceful Gazelle

God gave Melanie a flying opportunity she couldn't turn down. Although she'd decided she'd had enough of flight, God began transforming her fear into faith so she could go with Him to the high places.

At that time she was the cardiac care nursing supervisor of a large regional hospital. A famous pastor came to preach a revival at her church, and, after arriving in Oklahoma City, he suffered a major heart attack. Critically ill, he lay in her cardiac care unit for several days. Finally the family decided to have him flown back to Memphis on an Intensive Air Care Flight and insisted the only nurse they wanted to accompany him was Melanie.

"It didn't help that every time I walked in this man's hospital room the elderly pastor was praying that the plane would crash so he'd be with his wife who had died several years before," she says. This was a man with a reputation for always having his prayers answered.

Melanie didn't want to go and came up with numerous excuses, but the family, the doctor, and her own pastor put pressure on her, insisting no other nurse would do to monitor his multiple medications and IV drips on the intensive care flight. "I was literally sick at my stomach at the thought of having to fly to Memphis in a tiny plane," she says. "But I determined with the Lord that I wasn't going to live that way anymore. I was becoming like people I knew who didn't take trips with their families because of their fear of flying. So I told God I'd go if He would go with me and help me."

That afternoon, still anxious about the upcoming flight, she left her office and went down to the gift shop. First a ceramic angel holding a little rabbit caught her eye. Next she found a little open book that said, "Faith in God will hold you up when everything else falls." She bought the angel and the papier mâché book and put them on her desk, looking at them many times a day. *Faith in God will hold me up when everything else falls*, she thought. The angel reminded her that God sends His angels to take care of things—including intensive care flights and passengers! Her confidence grew a little, enough to board the plane.

In flight, she couldn't be preoccupied with her own fears because increased air pressure caused the patient's IV drips to double in frequency, which created a huge danger. Handling his medical crises while reminding herself during the entire flight that "Faith in God will hold me up when everything else falls," she made it to Memphis and then back to Oklahoma City. After that trip on the small ICU jet, Melanie felt she could make it on any airplane. The elderly pastor got back safely to Memphis and lived several more months, while she has enjoyed numerous flights since then. "My favorite place is still not on the top of an icy mountain slope with slick sticks [skis]," she says. But she's come a long way.

Who's in Control?

Flying in an airplane, strapped in a seatbelt, is the ultimate in having no control; and when the newspaper flashes the headline, "Human Error Behind Crash of Major Airlines Plane in Colombia" and goes on to describe the horrible crash that ended the lives of more than 160 people, it reminds us that we really aren't in control, that life is fragile. Driving our own cars or sitting in our living rooms, we have the illusion of control and safety. But as Lynn Parsley, a family counselor, says, "Control is an illusion, but a cherished one."

Even though statistics show that you are eighteen times safer flying in an airplane than you are taking a shower in your own home, still many people struggle with in-flight anxiety. When two commuter planes crashed a few months apart, even seasoned business travelers who logged thousands of miles a year in flight time got cold feet. Hundreds of them rented cars and drove long distances to avoid flying on commuter planes. Approximately half of passengers drink or take prescription pills to get through the flight. If we're not in control in the air, who is?

"All of our fears represent in some form, I believe, the fear of death, common to all of us," writes Elisabeth Elliot in *Keep a Quiet Heart*.

But is it our business to pray into what may happen tomorrow? It is a difficult and painful exercise which saps the strength and uses up the time given us *today*. Once we give ourselves up to God, shall we attempt to get hold of what can never belong to us—*tomorrow?* Our lives are His, our time's in His hand, He is Lord over what *will* happen, never mind what may happen. When we prayed 'Thy will be done,' did we suppose He did not hear us? He heard indeed, and daily makes our business His and partakes of our lives. If my life is once surrendered, all is well. Let me not grab it back, as though it were in peril in His hand but would be safer in *mine!*[4]

Bringing It Home

What to Do When Anxiety Strikes

If you experience anxiety when traveling by plane, train, car, or boat, try these suggestions:

Remember, wherever you are, God is there. I find the best course of action when flying is to put my life in His hands, as I do each day, but especially before a trip—remembering wherever I am, He is with me. Psalm 139:7–10 says:

> Where can I go from your Spirit?
>   Where can I flee from your presence?
> If I go up to the heavens, you are there;
> [that's good news if I fly on a small commuter plane!]
>   if I make my bed in the depths, you are there.
> If I rise on the wings of the dawn,
>   if I settle on the far side of the sea,
> [I hope, the boat or plane won't land there!]
> even there your hand will guide me,
>   your right hand will hold me fast.

What good news! No matter where we are, underneath are God's everlasting arms, and we can find peace on the journey.

Focus on God's Word while taking deep, slow breaths. Dwelling on God's Word fills us with faith and drives out fear. *Speaking* the words that remind us that God is our Protector is even better. Verses like "The Lord God is my strength, my personal bravery and my invincible army; He makes my feet like hinds' feet, and will make me to walk [and sometimes fly] . . . on high places" (Hab. 3:19, AMP) remind me that I can trust His grace and protection. Memorize several verses that bring you comfort and courage so they will be in your mind's "file cabinet," quickly retrievable in fearful situations. See "Lifesavers" Scriptures at the end of this chapter.

Pray specifically! I pray for ministering angels around the plane, the pilot, and all of us passengers. "For He will give His angels charge concerning you, to guard you in all your ways," good news when you're in the air (Ps. 91:11, NASB).

When Dorothy's son Richard was in Air Force training flying T-38s, he was so excited. He and the other pilots-in-training would fly in formation at extremely high speeds.

"I was just panicked for him," Dorothy says. In Arizona there were blue skies every day, and she knew they'd be up there flying. Worry totally preoccupied her mind.

During this anxious time, a friend visited for lunch and said: "Dorothy, I'm ashamed of you! Why are you worried about Richard? Don't you know God loves him a lot more than you do?" The friend suggested Dorothy pray that day for God to assign an angel to fly on his wing.

"I never worried again about Richard," says Dorothy. "I just pray each day for an angel to fly on the wing of his plane." Both flying in the Air Force and as a pilot for a major commercial airline, he has had close calls, flown in dense fog, snowstorms, and blizzards; but Dorothy knows the angel on his wing will bring him safely home.

Distract yourself with activity. Staying occupied while in flight is another practical stress-reducer. I take a new magazine or find one on board; I work on new articles or books-in-progress. I also take stationery and stamps in my briefcase and catch up on correspondence. I look forward to having a chat with a far-away friend on paper and getting it all ready to mail when we land. I stay so busy that I'm surprised when the pilot comes on the intercom to say we're almost there!

Remind yourself of the facts:

- You're safer in an airplane than in a car on a highway (or even your own bed). More people die in their beds than in airplanes.
- Your chance of perishing in an airline crash is one in ten million.
- Your chances of dying from a bee sting are greater than dying in a plane crash.
- You are eighteen times safer flying in a plane than you are taking a shower.

So enjoy your next flight!

Lifesavers and Worrybusters

What a God he is! How perfect in every way! All his promises prove true. He is a shield for everyone who hides behind him. For who is God except our Lord? Who but he is as a rock? He fills me with strength and protects me wherever I go. He gives me the surefootedness of a mountain goat upon the crags. He leads me safely along the top of the cliffs. He prepares me for battle and gives me strength to draw an iron bow! (Ps. 18:30–34, TLB)

Preserve sound judgment and discernment,
    do not let them out of your sight;
they will be life for you, an ornament to grace your neck.
Then you will go on your way in safety,
    and your foot will not stumble;
when you lie down, you will not be afraid;
    when you lie down, your sleep will be sweet.
    (Prov. 3:21–23)

Live under the protection of God Most High
    and stay in the shadow of God All-Powerful.
Then you will say to the LORD,
"You are my fortress, my place of safety;
    you are my God, and I trust you."
    (Ps. 91:1–2, *The Promise*)

Lord, you have been our dwelling place
    throughout all generations.
Before the mountains were born
    or you brought forth the earth and the world,
    from everlasting to everlasting you are God.
    (Ps. 90:1–2)
God will command his angels to protect you
    wherever you go.
They will carry you in their arms,
    and you won't hurt your feet on the stones.
    (Ps. 91:11, *The Promise*)
God is our refuge and strength,
    an ever-present help in trouble.
    (Ps. 46:1)

6

The Tornado Bag:
Overcoming Childhood Fears

Trust in the dark, trust in the light
trust at night, and trust in the morning.
—HANNAH WHITALL SMITH

Amy, a seven-year-old growing up in a small west-Texas town, went to sleep one April night as she did most spring evenings, with her jeans, shirt, and tennis shoes on. By the door she had placed her "tornado bag," an old green duffel bag containing her Bible, favorite photographs, a jar of peanut butter with crackers, and a flashlight.

"Don't worry. Your daddy is watching the storm," her mom reminded when she tucked her in. But that didn't keep Amy from worry and fear. As she lay in bed shivering, arms tight around her teddy bear on that warm spring evening, she kept her ear tuned to the beeping sound on the television that signaled a tornado was coming.

The town lay right in a tornado path or "draw," and from March through June, at least three times a week the whole town was on alert because of severe storms that frequently blew through the area. Many of those nights more than five hundred people, including Amy's family, would crowd into the community storm cellar, which was the underground level of the elementary school where her father served as principal.

That night Amy was almost asleep when her father rushed in, grabbed her, and carried her to the car. The television beeped a high-pitched signal. Amy clutched her little brown poodle puppy and tornado bag to her chest. Just before her dad put her in the back seat, a softball-size hailstone hit his forearm, splitting it open. Amy watched in horror as blood spurted out from his gash all over her jeans, but it didn't slow her dad down. He had to unlock the school so the townspeople could go in for shelter.

They were down in the basement with five hundred other people for a short while, and then everyone started filing up the stairs, thinking the storm's danger had blown over. But when Amy's dad looked out the window, he saw telephone poles flying through the air and masses of debris whirling. The tornado had turned around, split into three funnels, and was bringing more destruction in its path.

⋅⋙◉⋘⋅

*The lens of fear magnifies
the size of the uncertainty.*
—Charles Swindoll

⋅⋙◉⋘⋅

Amy felt absolutely numb that what they'd feared for so long was happening. Amazingly, when they returned to their home later that night, it wasn't damaged. But from that fear, others grew. She began having nightmares about tornadoes and thunderstorms. She imagined she saw men at her window. She wouldn't go to a friend's house to spend the night unless they had a basement or storm shelter.

As Amy grew into adolescence, her fears didn't dissipate; they matured. She was afraid of being rejected, of failing, of not being perfect. On the outside she acted happy, took part in school activities, and achieved good grades. But on the inside, she was fearful and tormented.

"I had a huge private fear of not succeeding at what God called me to do and of marrying the wrong man," Amy says.

But she couldn't talk about her anxiety with anyone. Her loving Christian family was very private about feelings. They *especially* didn't talk about their fears. Amy felt she had to be strong and brave for her gentle, somewhat insecure mom. Her dad thought being afraid of storms or anything else was silly. He expected Amy to be logical about things. So her fears remained hidden.

Post-traumatic Stress Syndrome

Everybody is fearful or anxious at one time or another, especially those who grow up as Amy did, where the threat of destruction is a constant in childhood. And most of us carry a few childhood fears into our adulthood. But people whose anxiety becomes paralyzing can usually trace the onset to some stressful or traumatic event. In Amy's case, that event was childhood sexual abuse she experienced at the age of five at the kindergarten/daycare she attended while her mother worked each afternoon.

"Being a withdrawn child in a private family that stuffed feelings, and being a perfectionist, I closed everything off even though the abuse was devastating," she says. "My parents didn't know anything about the abuse."

Experts say memories of abuse are often repressed. "These memories may seem to go away, but the emotion doesn't," says Dr. Steve Gold, who specializes in child and adolescent psychology. "Instead the fear is like free-floating anxiety that becomes attached to something external like tornadoes. It's okay to be afraid of storms or strangers, yet it's hard to face the betrayal of trust and shame from the abuse."

The effects are similar to soldiers returning from battle who experience post-traumatic stress disorder (PTSD) in which their whole sense of control is destroyed. On the outside, Amy tried to maintain a sense of normalcy and control; on the inside, her fears escalated. In addition, Amy, like many women who are abused, experienced continual guilt that floated underneath all she did. This guilt, which stems from the misbelief that "If I'd been really good enough or strong enough, I could have kept the abuse from happening," led to low self-esteem that drove her constant attempts to be thin enough or perfect enough to please people in her life.

Childhood Fears

Just like keeping a tattered teddy bear from childhood, many times when we don't have the resources to face and resolve childhood conflicts and emotions, we drag them right into adult life. For example, a child who learned to fear rejection will often experience loneliness and isolation in adulthood. A child caught up in the performance trap by parents who were never satisfied with his or her achievement will tend to be perfectionistic and self-condemning as an adult.

In Amy's case, the childhood fears that reached all the way back to her "tornado bag" nights were alive and well and kept her from moving on with her life. As Robert McGee says, "Fear, in one form or another, usually is why people continue their childhood patterns rather than to 'put childish ways behind them.'"[1]

In college Amy met and married a singer with a Christian band who came into town and swept her off her feet. When the young husband's perfectionism demanded that she look like she walked out of a Hollywood movie, which required working out twice a day and losing weight (when she weighed only one hundred pounds), it intensified her fear of failure and rejection.

"I was so naive; I had no concept that abuse could happen in my marriage, but it started out as emotional and verbal, progressing during the five years we were married to physical abuse," Amy says. She was afraid of not being thin enough and pretty enough for her husband to love her and developed anorexia and bulimia in the process of trying desperately to please him.

The abuse cycle fed her fear of being rejected. When Amy broke emotionally and physically and the marriage failed, she feared God couldn't love her and that people wouldn't accept her. She also feared the Christian community's rejection. And although she felt God had some purpose for her, she was afraid she'd never be restored enough to find it.

God Steps In

And then God intervened and picked Amy up. He began a process of restoration that is continuing. After several years of extensive counseling, Bible study, and growth in her Christian life, Amy worked through many of her fears and gained some degree of emotional health. She also met a wonderful man, and they married and had a daughter, now two years old. Layer after layer, the healing process continued.

However, when her husband was away on business trips as a pharmaceutical rep, Amy became insanely jealous. "We were happily married, so I couldn't understand this intense, irrational jealousy that kept me from trusting John," she says. She pictured him with other women on his travels; she worried that he'd leave her although he was faithful and loved her dearly. She was consumed by jealousy.

One day she got on her face before God and cried out, "Why am I so jealous? Why can't I get past this?" She begged God to free her.

A few days later she was at home alone and got a solicitation call from a woman doing a survey for a telemarketing firm. "Normally I would hang up, but I was lonely. John had been gone for several days. So I talked to the lady." One question concerned employment and when asked if she worked, Amy replied that she was a freelance writer.

"Who do you write for?" the woman inquired. When Amy named a Christian ministry, the lady said she was also a Christian, and they struck up a conversation. Then before hanging up the woman suddenly said, "Would you meet me for coffee? I know this is unusual, but I'd really like to get together with you to talk. My name is Doris Wafer." Before Amy knew it, the date and place to meet the woman were set.

The minute Amy hung up the phone she was petrified about having to go meet a stranger. However, when the day finally came, she found herself in the coffee shop waiting to meet this mystery woman. Suddenly, the most beautiful, radiant older woman she had ever seen walked in and sat down across from Amy. Silver-haired and apparently in her late sixties, the woman had glassy blue eyes that sparkled with life. Over coffee she shared her story, emphasizing to Amy, "You've got to hear me about this fear. You've got to hear what God did." She even repeated the story, urging her, "Please listen closely."

Doris related that when she was in her fifties, she was diagnosed with terminal cancer. Lying in her hospital bed, with only weeks to live, she began asking God, "Why me?" She had been a Christian for years and had loved and served Him for as long as she could remember—and she just didn't understand why she had to die of cancer. She had so much yet to do!

Doris's family had a long history of family members dying from cancer, including her husband. As she lay in the hospital bed questioning God and asking Him to heal her, she had a vision. Doris saw herself standing before the cross holding something in her hand, and then she heard the Lord say, "Doris, I can deal with the disease—the cancer—but I can't deal with the fear. That's yours to lay down." The Holy Spirit began to impress upon her that she had harbored such a fear of cancer that her faith was literally paralyzed by her fears.

Suddenly Doris saw herself take what was in her hands, put it in a box, tie a pink bow around it, and place it at the foot of the cross. Then she heard herself say aloud, "I lay all my fears at Your feet, Jesus." She was completely healed of cancer that day, restored to total health, and had been free of cancer for ten years.

This woman had no idea of the fears Amy had struggled with, but through her story God seemed to be saying, "Amy, I can deal with whatever comes in your life, like John's traveling or people rejecting you, but *you must lay down your fears*."

"I realized I had grabbed hold of the fear of rejection so tightly, I couldn't get away from it," she says. That was underneath the insane jealousy. She'd tried everything within her knowledge of prayer, listening to tapes, memorizing Scriptures, and counseling.

Laying Down the Tornado Bag

"But God was saying that *I* had to let go of the fear," says Amy. "He wouldn't make me; that was my choice, just as it was Doris's choice to hold on to or give God her fear of cancer. It was an act of my will. But I understood now that my fear was keeping me from operating in faith—which motivated me to lay it down!"

At that point, Amy gave God the tornado bag she had held onto all those stormy nights as a child and had carried throughout her life. Filled with the fear of rejection and all the other anxieties God brought to her mind, Amy laid the old bag at the feet of Jesus. And she knew then that she could trust God to handle all the uncontrollable events and storms that might blow through her and her family's life.

The Root Is Removed

That was three years ago. Amy met the elderly woman one more time to chat, but then when she tried to contact her, there was no one at the number who answered to "Doris Wafer," and no other listing could be found for her. She even tried to contact the church she said she attended but had no luck locating her. Doris remained a mystery.

Every time the fear that her husband was going to reject her or be unfaithful came up in her thoughts, Amy released it immediately. Once the fear dissipated, more insights came. The Lord showed her husband a picture of a big root, and the root was rejection. There was a blanket laying on top of it that was her fear, and three prongs held the blanket on securely: unforgiveness, self-hatred, and self-rejection caused by the childhood abuse. With the blanket of fear removed, Amy was able to deal with the memories of abuse, forgive her abuser, and come into more freedom than she'd ever known. As her trust in God began to increase, *faith* became the source of her decisions and actions and the foundation of her life instead of anxiety.

⤛❍⤜

FAITH never fails.
It is a miracle worker.
It looks beyond all boundaries,
transcends all limitations,
penetrates all obstacles,
and sees the goal.
—*Orison S. Marden*

⤛❍⤜

"It's a wonder—I marvel at what God has done, and it's *wonderful* to be out of the grips of fear because it was such torment inside," says Amy. Since overcoming the fears that had paralyzed her life for years, Amy and her husband now present seminars on marriage called "The SuperNatural Marriage—The Call to Intimacy" that include a session on overcoming fear. Amy has a special passion for helping other women.

Bringing It Home

God can help you deal with your problems and overcome anything, but it is your part to lay your fears at His feet. What specific fears do you need to put in a box tied with a bow and give to God?

How to Overcome Your Fear

Identify and write down what you're afraid of or the overwhelming problem you're carrying. "God can and will provide whatever we need to get beyond our painful emotions, but only if we are willing to be honest about them," says McGee.[2]

Discuss your list with a trusted friend or counselor. Then give your fears and worries to God with some concrete gesture. You could put your list in a small box or bag and keep it as a reminder that on this date you laid down your fears. One prayer group has a "God Box." Each week as they pray about their lives and problems, they put slips of paper with the things they have given to the Lord in the "God Box" as a reminder that they are *His*. Then when thoughts about these concerns recur, remind yourself that you have given these to God; they are not yours to hash over or pick up.

If anxiety persists, seek help. Remember that some anxiety, panic, and fearfulness are components of clinical depression. In many cases depression has a biochemical root (perhaps coexisting with other emotional and spiritual roots) and can be greatly relieved by medication and therapy. Seek help with a licensed professional counselor or pastoral counseling in addition to continuing your own devotional life, Bible study, and applying the suggestions in this book. Also, consider a weekly support group using as a format the "Questions for Discussion and Reflection" in the back of this book. Small groups are particularly effective for those with anxiety. We often think we're the only one who is afraid, so there is healing and tremendous support in dealing with these issues in a group setting.

All through the Bible God says, "Fear not . . . ," so you can believe and receive His promises and blessings. If you fear not, *God will fulfill His promises.* There's a promise that follows every time God says, "Fear not." For example, in Joshua 8:1 God told Joshua: "Do not fear or be dismayed. Take all the people of war with you, and arise, go up to Ai; see, I have given into your hand the king of Ai, his people, his city, and his land" (NASB). Just as He had commanded Joshua earlier, God wanted him to be strong, vigorous, and very courageous (see Josh. 1:9). God promised His presence and empowering help. Look up other "Fear nots" and notice what God promises following His command: 1 Chronicles 22:13; Luke 12:32; Deuteronomy 1:21 (see below).

Lifesavers and Worrybusters

Have I not commanded you? Be strong and courageous! Do not tremble or be dismayed, for the LORD your God is with you wherever you go. (Josh. 1:9, NASB)

He alone is my Rock, my rescuer, defense and fortress—why then should I be tense with fear when troubles come? (Ps. 62:6, TLB)

The Lord will protect you
  and keep you safe from all dangers.
The Lord will protect you
  now and always wherever you go.
      (Ps. 121:7–8, *The Promise*)

Be strong and courageous. Do not be afraid or discouraged.
(1 Chron. 22:13)

"Do not tremble and do not be afraid;
Have I not long since announced it to you and declared it?
And you are My witnesses.
Is there any God besides Me,
Or is there any other Rock?
I know of none." (Isa. 44:8, NASB)

Don't fall into the trap of being a coward—trust the LORD, and
  you will be safe. (Prov. 29:25, *The Promise*)

From the ends of the earth I call to you,
  I call as my heart grows faint;
  lead me to the rock that is higher than I.

For you have been my refuge,
  a strong tower against the foe. (Ps. 61:2–3)

The LORD your God is with you,
  he is mighty to save.

He will take great delight in you,
  he will quiet you with his love,
  he will rejoice over you with singing. (Zeph. 3:17)

The joy of the LORD is your strength. (Neh. 8:10)

Trust in the LORD and do good . . .
Delight yourself in the LORD
  and he will givev you the desires of your heart.
Commit your way to the LORD;
  trust in him and he will do this:
He will make your righteousness shine like the dawn,
  the justice of your cause like the noonday sun. (Ps. 37:3–6)

7

Five P's for Handling Panic: Making Peace Your Pattern

Fear not, Christian; Jesus is with Thee. In all thy fiery trials His presence is both thy comfort and safety; He will never leave one whom He has chosen for His own. "Fear not, for I am with Thee," is His sure word of promise to His chosen ones in the furnace of affliction.
—CHARLES SPURGEON

Esther helped her elderly patient settle into a bed in the outpatient oncology center where she worked as a nurse. She chatted comfortably while gathering supplies and preparing the medication for the patient's chemotherapy.

All of Esther's patients were favorites, but this woman held a special place in her heart. Even after twenty years of nursing, Esther prayed each morning for God's wisdom and help in treating her patients.

"Let me check your IV site," Esther said, making sure the needle was securely in the vein. Then she read each page of the chart to be sure she had all the information she needed. Since the platelet counts were low, Esther called over to the oncology doctor to verify the treatment. He couldn't be reached, but the nurse assured her the doctor had ordered the chemo and two units of blood. Esther turned back to her patient and gently took her hand. Then the medications flowed into her vein.

Every morning as Esther spent some quiet time with the Lord, she asked for God's guidance with her patients, especially for protection of their veins and any possible dangerous side effects. This morning was no different, and she had confidence in His help.

As the last of the chemotherapy was being given, the phone rang. The doctor said, "Whatever you do, *don't* give the patient chemotherapy today. I guess you saw that her counts are too low."

"I already did," Esther said.

"How could you be so incompetent?" he screamed. "You'll probably be responsible for this patient's death!"

When her husband, Tim, picked Esther up a few hours later to drive to an out-of-state retreat, she was sick with worry. Her stomach was knotted tightly, and the doctor's tirade still rang in her ears as she thought, *I'll probably go to jail if this patient dies.* This is a nightmare that every nurse hopes and prays will never happen to her—that *her* mistake could kill a patient.

All the way down to the Texas conference center, Esther agonized, "God, how can I pray over my patients and trust You and then have this happen?"

If she dies, I don't know what I'll do. Even if I don't go to jail, I'll lose my nursing license, she thought, her faith shaken to the core. *Can I really trust God at all?* Fear tightened around her until she felt she would be sick. *She's so precious . . . not just a patient, but a friend.* The fear of her patient's dying was overwhelming. She couldn't shake it, not even with her husband's encouragement.

By the time she and Tim arrived at the conference center, Esther was a wreck and deep in the pit of despair. Even though it was hot outside, she felt cold. When she ran into Bill, the retreat speaker and an old friend, the story poured out. "I may be responsible for a patient's death," Esther cried. "How can I even concentrate on the seminars when my patient may be in danger?"

"I think you're at just the right place. Come to the first session on worry," Bill encouraged her. After settling their suitcases in the room, Esther reluctantly filed into the room with friends from church, doubtful there would be anything said that could quell her fears. Her thoughts swirled with anxiety, and her heart wouldn't stop racing.

In the seminar, Bill explained that he had always struggled with worry until he discovered the "Four P's" in Philippians 4:6–8: "Be anxious for nothing, but in everything by prayer and supplication with thanksgiving let your requests be made known to God. And the peace of God, which surpasses all comprehension, shall guard your hearts and your minds in Christ Jesus. Finally, brethren, whatever is true, whatever is honorable, whatever is right, whatever is pure, whatever is lovely . . . if there is any excellence and if anything worthy of praise, let your mind dwell on these things" (NASB).

I know these verses by heart, Esther thought. *I don't see how hearing them again can help.*

"You see," Bill explained, "whenever God commands us to *do something*—in this case, to be anxious for nothing—He always follows with *how to do it*.

"The first *P* is to *pray* about what worries you and consciously give it to God.

"The second *P* is to *praise* Him for what He will do in the situation. Thank God for the person or situation causing you worry and anxiety.

"The third *P* is to receive God's *peace*. It's a promise. If you've prayed about the worry, given it to God with thanksgiving, then He will move in on your mind and heart with peace through Christ Jesus, because of His work in you."

As Esther continued taking notes, what the speaker said began to make sense. Her fear was just as oppressive as when they arrived, but she listened intently as he sketched on the board the remaining *P*.

"The fourth *P* is what to do next," the speaker continued. "Focus your mind on *positive thoughts* about God. Focus on praising Him, on all the positive, wonderful things about His character instead of being preoccupied with negative thoughts and the 'What ifs?' Center your mind on God's goodness."

⊶⫥◉⫤⊷

Fear God
and you will have nothing else to fear.
—Anonymous

⊶⫥◉⫤⊷

Applying the Four P's

Following the seminar, Esther returned to her room and had a long talk with God. "I've always been able to count on everything in Your Word. I'm going to put these Four P's into practice, regardless of how I feel," she said. She prayed through the Four P's, at first mechanically, and gave the whole situation *and* the patient she was so worried about to God. Thanking Him for this trial was difficult, but when Esther did, she experienced a few brief minutes of peace.

However, five minutes later the panic was back again. Over and over again she gave her fears to God, thanked Him the best she could for how He was working in her heart and in the situation, and consciously focused on His character, His promises, and His truth. Each time, Esther received a longer respite of peace. As she continued praying in this way, the little blocks of time without fear gradually grew from five minutes to ten and then twenty.

But the next morning when Esther awoke, her heart was beating wildly, and the anxiety was back with full force. *She's going to die, and I'm going to prison*, she thought. *Who will care for Tim and my four girls?* She got down on her knees and prayed through the Four P's of Philippians, and this time when the anxiety returned, it wasn't with as much agony. Throughout the second day and while taking notes in other sessions, Esther kept giving God her fears, offering her thanks, centering her mind on His faithfulness. The moments without anxiety grew.

"By Sunday, the peace I was experiencing was so incredible, I couldn't *make* myself worry," she said. Before, when she thought of the situation, she was filled with stark terror. But in those three days, she had moved from despair and fear to absolute confidence in God—whatever the outcome.

Through this experience, God was teaching her that she had to trust Him, not the circumstances. And, amazingly, in the next few weeks, she saw her patient not only improve; her cancer went into remission. Although the doctor never admitted that the final dose of chemotherapy had helped turn her condition around, Esther knew God had been at work in her patient's life as well as her own.

A Wave of Trials

Applying the Four P's became a truth Esther started living in other areas of her life besides her nursing, and God used that passage in Philippians to steady her faith during some extremely rough storms in their lives that lay ahead. Trials and tragedy often seem to come in waves in our lives, one after the other, just as they did in Esther's family. During the next several years, two of their four daughters began to seek enjoyment in worldly pleasures that ended in their second daughter becoming pregnant out of wedlock.

Esther felt a tremendous burden and concern for her daughters. "It was only in the power of being in God's presence," said Esther, "that He'd lift off the tremendous burdens and anxieties I felt for our girls." As she gave God her concerns, she also thanked Him: "I don't understand, but I trust You; Donna is in rebellion, but I thank You that You can use it for Your glory and even the pregnancy to draw her to Yourself," she prayed.

Donna elected to allow a Christian couple to adopt her baby, and, as it turned out, they agreed to keep Tim and Esther informed about significant happenings in the baby's life. God worked miraculously, and they saw His hand. He even brought Donna back to a relationship with Christ. And this little granddaughter, now a five-year-old, gave her heart to Christ this year.

The next wave of difficulty was Tim's mother's massive stroke, which meant that Esther had to resign her nursing position and care for her full-time at their home, a twenty-four-hour job full of stress and exhaustion. The P's had now grown to *five* because verse 9 says, "Practice these things; and the God of peace shall be with you," and Esther was definitely *practicing these things!* When she prayed through the Five P's, God showed her that instead of being consumed with the stress of caring for a totally helpless elderly person, she could pray for the world *and* for their girls at the same time. Then after nine months of this duty, her husband was suddenly diagnosed with colon cancer.

Five days after Tim's surgery she attended the Tumor Board meeting and heard her husband's doctors discuss the lymph node involvement and the need for chemotherapy. The guilt was overwhelming. Leaving the meeting in tears, she drove home and began to cry out to the Lord with her burden of guilt: "Lord, every morning I was with You—I've worked with cancer patients for years. I should have seen the signs. Why didn't You let me know?"

But immediately as she began to praise God for what He would do, He led her to open her Bible and start reading the next chapter of Job she had been reading daily. There it was! Job 14:5: "[Man's] days are determined. The number of his months is with Thee" (NASB).

It was as if God said, "Who do you think you are? I am the One sovereign over life and death. *I* determine Tim's days. You must trust Me in what I am doing." And just as always, when she practiced giving her worries about Tim to God and thanking Him, His peace began to flood her heart and mind. Little did she know this special verse would again give her great comfort eight months later.

Full trust in the Lord
turns anxiety to REST.
—Anonymous

A Daughter Comes "Home"

One night after Tim's surgery their daughter Diane came by the hospital and dissolved in tears alone with her mother. It was obvious God was softening her heart. Two months later she came by the house and asked, "Can I move back home again?"

Since they had put Tim's mother in the nursing home so that Esther could care for Tim in his recovery, Diane's room was open again. "Do you think Steve and I could study the Bible with you and Dad?" was her next request a week later. Five months of Monday nights followed, in which they studied the Word together with Diane and her boyfriend. On one of the last nights, they had a chance to talk about salvation. "If something happened and either of you were face-to-face with Christ, would you be assured of your salvation?" Tim and Esther asked them both. A lively discussion ensued.

Diane answered with verse after verse: how she knew she was forgiven of her sin because of Christ's death on the cross in her place; she knew it was not based on anything of her doing but His drawing her to Himself because of *His grace*. Esther and Tim were so grateful for this discussion in the weeks that followed.

They had no way of knowing that it would be one of their last Bible studies together. Only three weeks later Diane's car was hit head-on by a drunk driver. When Diane didn't arrive home from Steve's house, her father and Steve both went out looking for her. Esther stayed home and "prayed up a storm," hoping they would find her with a flat tire or minor breakdown.

"Suddenly as I prayed, I saw a clear picture of God's hands," Esther says. "And there in His hands was Diane." *She's OK. She's all right.* Only moments later she got the call from the hospital that Diane had been in a serious wreck. Their daughter died later that night, following surgery for two punctures in her heart and massive internal bleeding.

"I had to be alone with the Lord," she said, her heart breaking over Diane's death. "God, I know You have been perfect in every situation—but I don't know if I can praise or thank You yet."

"Yes, you can," God seemed to say, and at that instant He flooded her mind with memories: the "love" letter He had prompted her to write and leave on Diane's pillow only the day before, the months of Monday night Bible study, the togetherness and fun they'd experienced that very night at dinner with their four girls. Diane had not only come back home to live but had truly "come home" to Christ that August.

Finally, Job 14:5 raced into her mind, "[Man's] days are determined." Deep peace of His sovereignty in Diane's life and death began to settle over her.

The pattern of Philippians 4, casting all her cares and feelings on God and thanking Him in the midst of struggles, had cultivated a deep intimacy that enabled Esther to draw close to God even in this terrible tragedy. "Draw near to God and He will draw near to you" (James 4:8, NASB) is a *promise* that Esther found true. In the midst of missing Diane so much, of feeling a gut-wrenching desire to hold her in the weeks and months that followed, God's incredible peace was always side by side with the pain.

"Be anxious for nothing" covers a lot of ground. It covers fear, guilt, anger, all the things that cause anxiety to well up. This anxiety is Satan's ballpark. With it, he tries to defeat the Christian because we proclaim God's glory. You can't proclaim God's goodness and greatness when you're scared stiff or wrapped up in anxiety or panic. Yet glorifying God is at the core of our purpose for being: "You are a chosen race, a royal priesthood, a holy nation, a people for God's own possession, that you may proclaim the excellencies of Him who has called you out of darkness into His marvelous light" (1 Pet. 2:9, NASB).

By handling anxiety-producing situations with the Five P's of Philippians, *God*—instead of the circumstances—becomes our focus, and *peace* replaces panic. *Wonder* replaces worry—wonder at His awesome peace that has filled our minds. Wonder at God's faithfulness and provision, so you can "Celebrate God all day, every day. . . . revel in him!" (Phil. 4:4, *The Message*).

A. W. Tozer calls this the "astonished wonder" that is at the heart of true worship. This sense of "spiritual astonishment" happens among men and women when the Holy Spirit is present, working in their lives, just as it happened in Esther's life.

Bringing It Home

We each have different "panic buttons" and certain experiences that can shake our trust in God. Sometimes it is a single calamitous event, like the death of a spouse or job loss. Other times misfortune comes as it did in Job's life—an earthquake of tragedy plus aftershocks of difficulty and pain, wherein his fortune was lost, his sons and daughters died, he was afflicted with boils as he sat in the ashes, and his wife suggested he curse God and die.

For Esther the possibility of a patient dying because of her actions triggered overwhelming anxiety. No matter what *your* particular panic buttons are, the truth of God's Word can turn your worry to wonder and free you from anxiety.

The Five P's are not a magic formula, but they *do work* because God's Word is true, and when we put it into practice, *life happens*—we come out of darkness and fear into light and hope.

When Your "Panic Button" Is Pushed

The moment anxiety hits, go right to God. Pull away wherever you are and get into God's presence. No matter where you are—at work, driving down the freeway, even in the midst of a conversation—take the worry to Him *instead of engaging it in your mind* and thinking of all the terrible things that could happen.

When something happens that causes fear or anxiety, we have a tendency to blame God for allowing us to go through the difficulty. When we blame God and turn away from Him,

Satan has a heyday with our thoughts. Our mind becomes his playground. That's why we're to "take captive every thought to make it obedient to Christ" (2 Cor. 10:5).

Don't leave out the thanksgiving! No matter what the situation, begin to thank God, including how He's blessed you recently:

- How He's drawing you to Him through the worry
- What He is going to do in the situation
- How you're going to grow in the situation or difficulty
- How God is going to reveal Himself in that need or concern, etc.

As you thank God and begin to praise Him, you're choosing to focus on *Him* instead of the situation, and it delights God's heart. All of life tries to pull you down into the circumstance, but when you praise God, then He blesses you with the ability to cope victoriously with the problem. At the same time, Satan and his discouragement and doubts will *flee* from you. Thanksgiving is powerful—don't leave it out!

"Thanksgiving gives effect to prayer," said Robert Jamieson, "and frees us from anxious carefulness by making all God's dealings a matter for praise, not merely for resignation, much less murmuring. Peace is the companion of thanksgiving."[1]

Persist and don't give up! If you have prayed through the Five P's and given your worry to God and it comes back a few minutes later, don't give up! Remember that the bigger or heavier the anxiety or problem, the more times you may need to give it to God until it's really released. If the fear recurs, don't say "Well, this isn't working." Instead, stop and give your worry to God again. Each time you will get a little more victory. Your peace will increase until your mind is totally at rest concerning the matter. *Rest* means mental and spiritual tranquillity, freedom from all worries. And that's when the creative solution or revelation of what you're to do will come to mind. There is *nothing* too hard for God!

"Claiming" God's peace is a matter of yielding to Him and receiving His peace. The battleground is the mind, and that's

why Philippians 4:7 says, "The peace of God, which surpasses all comprehension, shall guard your hearts and your minds in Christ Jesus" (NASB).

Peace is not what you conjure up to make yourself feel better about the situation or positive self-talk, but claiming the peace of Almighty God—a peace we cannot fathom or measure—will transform your very thoughts! Christ's whole nature is peace; He is the Prince of Peace. As *The Message*'s translation of that verse says, "Before you know it, a sense of God's wholeness, everything coming together for good, will come and settle you down. It's wonderful what happens when Christ displaces worry at the center of your life."

When we give God a worry or a person, He doesn't promise to remove the problem. (He certainly can intervene, however, and often does.) When Jesus said, "I came that they might have life, and have it abundantly," He did not mean that we won't have problems, but that He will give us the power and peace to live abundantly in the midst of adversity. And one of the ways He does that is to take the fears and worries we lay at the cross and give us His peace to cope with the situation.

Take off your dark glasses and look for God working in your situation! "The night is about over, dawn is about to break. Be up and awake to what God is doing!" (Rom. 13:12, *The Message*). When you fret and worry, it's like wearing dark glasses. You shut out the light and can't *see* what God is doing on your behalf or how He's moving. Then you miss the joy. Fear and anxiety also keep us from learning what God is trying to teach us through the experience. But if you're choosing to offer thanks to God and looking for things to praise Him for, you will see His loving hand at every turn—which will change your worry to wonder.

Let the Five P's become a way of life. "Practice these things" and use them every day in the small anxieties and the larger ones. As you do, giving your worries to God will become second nature. Just as soldiers in warfare practice the maneuvers and strategies to be ready to use them in combat, *practice* these Five P's so you'll be ready when your personal battle comes:

PRAY
PRAISE
PEACE
POSITIVE THOUGHTS
PRACTICE . . . PRACTICE . . . PRACTICE

It was *practicing* these truths over the years that changed Esther from a worrier to a prayer warrior who walks in God's peace and joy as a daily lifestyle, regardless of what challenges she faces. It has also enabled her to share her story with hundreds of women and see God work. Through Diane's death and the healing and comfort Esther and her husband experienced, God opened up countless opportunities for them to minister to young people and grieving people of all ages.

Through Diane's death, Sean (Donna's boyfriend and father of her baby) gave his heart to Christ, and he and Donna were married in April of 1994. God blessed them with a son in August 1995. Tim recovered from cancer and continued his associate pastor role at their church. And the Monday night Bible study continued with some of Diane's old friends and her sisters' friends, including those she came to know in her time of rebellion. Quite a few of them have come to know Christ.

To help you practice the Five P's, carry a card with you and put another one on the refrigerator with the words *Pray, Praise, Peace, Positive Thoughts, Practice* and the verses on it to remind you every day to release your worries to God. As you make them a part of your lifestyle, you'll find the Five D's—doubt, depression, despond, dread, and disease—will disappear. It's in the *practice* that the truth of Philippians 4:6–9 will move from your head to your heart, that the joy of the Lord will be the strength you need—not just to survive in the situation, but to worship God with an astonished sense of wonder and enjoy Him victoriously right in the midst of it.

8

Soaring with Your Talents: Overcoming Fear of Failure

Part of the Christian style of life involves a sponta-neity in which we lose our fear of failure and move out in the light of the guidance that we have.
—KEITH MILLER, *THE EDGE OF ADVENTURE*

Have you ever been afraid to fail? Whether anxiety before a big exam or job interview, whether a fear of public speaking or painting a picture, we've all experienced the nervousness, shaky hands, dry mouth, and anxious thoughts that accompany this fear. Sometimes we're afraid to say a prayer aloud in a group, teach a Bible study, or even ask a question in a Sunday School class.

I remember a woman I met who was a librarian and truly loved books. In fact, she informed me, she was working on a master's degree in creative writing. "I have a children's book I've written that I wish I could get published," she said one day when she found out I was a writer.

"Did you write a proposal and send it out?" I asked.

"No, I was afraid it would be rejected. I couldn't stand failing like that," she answered sadly.

This woman had a burning interest in writing, had taken courses for five years, and even had written articles in addition to the children's book. Yet her fears kept her from taking the next step—sending her work off for publication.

It reminds me of the cartoon in "The Family Circus" newspaper strip by Bill Keane in which two kids are peering inside a grand piano. The little girl instructs the small boy, "There are millions of songs in there, but you hafta' punch the right keys to get them out."

God gives us inspiration—great ideas, gifts and talents, words to write, and songs to play—but we have to apply the perspiration, even risking rejection and failure along the way.

Everyone is gifted. God created each of us with a combination of gifts and talents, or what I call "strengths" (an inner ability, something that can be displayed in a performance or used in a business, ministry, or creative situation). Perhaps you are the one who thinks of creative solutions to problems. Maybe you can organize a big event or teach a Bible study. Music may be your gift, or encouragement or compassionate serving.

Whatever the gift, we must pick that strength and pursue it. We also all have weaknesses; but if we focus on our weaknesses and failures, they begin to smother our strengths.

◦═◗◖═◦

He only fails
who never attempts.
—Anonymous

◦═◗◖═◦

When God Smiles

One of my favorite movies is *Chariots of Fire*, which tells the story of Eric Little, Scottish missionary to China and Olympic runner. In one scene, Eric's sister, standing on a green Scottish hillside, is scolding him for not being at the mission enough because of his daily running practice, preparing for the Olympic trials. "I believe that God made me for a purpose—for China.

"He also made me fast," he tells Jenny. "When I run, I feel His pleasure."

Similarly, when we use the gifts and talents God gives us—whether it's running, composing music, writing, teaching, coordinating events, or directing a business—we feel God's smile. We sense His pleasure, and we are filled with pure joy. Also, when we are using the gifts God gave us, we operate in a maximum of effectiveness and a minimum of weariness because we are doing what He made us for.

I believe that a big part of our purpose on earth is connected to these particular gifts and talents God has entrusted to us. But often, because of fear of failure, we do not use them. Remember the parable of the talents? A man gave five thousand coins to one servant, two thousand to the second, and one thousand to the third. Then he left the country. When he came back and checked on how his servants had done, he praised and rewarded the first servant, who had doubled his money. The second said, "Master, I made a 50 percent profit on your money," and he was also rewarded.

⊹━◉⊂━⊹

All these gifts were inspired by the same Spirit:
—Leading and motivating people
—Art talent
—Writing poetry
—The ability to make money
—Creative ability in any field
—Organization and administration
People skills
—Gifts of mercy, teaching, and encouragement
—Musical talent

⊹━◉⊂━⊹

But the next servant said, "Master, here's your money safe and sound. I kept it hidden in the cellar. To tell you the truth, I was a little afraid. I know you have high standards and hate sloppiness and don't suffer fools gladly."

He said, "You're right. . . . Why didn't you at least invest the money in securities so I would have gotten a little interest on it?" So he took the money from him and gave it to the productive servant who doubled his talent.

They said, "But Master, he already has double . . ."

He said, "That's what I mean: Risk your life and get more than you ever dreamed of. Play it safe and end up holding the bag" (Luke 19:11–27, *The Message*).

Battling a Fear of Failure

You may think that only people without talent are scared to step out and try something new. But even when a person is gifted and prepared to do a project, the fear of failure can paralyze her efforts.

Katherine, an artist, heard a message several years ago on what Jesus really suffered at crucifixion. She was struck by what the actual experience at the cross must have been. It also made her think about all the paintings she'd seen of the crucifixion. She searched for weeks in art museums and books to find such an image.

"I'd studied art all my life, and the more I looked the more I realized there was nothing painted of the crucifixion like what I heard in the message," Katherine says. She couldn't get free of those thoughts and kept asking God, "Lord, why hasn't this ever been painted? You've had such spiritual people, such gifted people."

God seemed to answer her, "It's for you to do."

The breath left her as Katherine contemplated the enormity of such a painting. But she dove into the research and preparation process. For the next four months, she studied Scriptures, paintings, photos, and compiled information from the library and the art museum reading room. It was a wonderful time, blessed with a sense of closeness with God.

But as her research was completed and it was time to start the painting, she started looking at her own inability to paint such a work. Her fear of failure paralyzed her day after day. At the same time, it was as though God stopped talking to her.

"After the richness of what I'd shared with God, the two-month silence that followed was frightening," Katherine says.

She started scrambling, searching in her quiet times in the Bible, taking more detailed notes in church, trying to figure out what was wrong. One day she felt so alone she prayed from Psalm 51, "Do not . . . take your Holy Spirit from me."

She was led to the story of the fig tree Jesus told in Luke 13:

> A man had a fig tree growing in his vineyard. One day he went out to pick some figs, but he didn't find any. So he said to the gardener, "For three years I have come looking for figs on this tree, and I haven't found any yet. Chop it down! Why should it take up space?"

> The gardener answered, "Master, leave it for another year. I'll dig around it and put some manure on it to make it grow. Maybe it will have figs on it next year. If it doesn't, you can have it cut down" (*The Promise*).

Meditating on that passage, Katherine felt God was saying, "You are the fig tree." She realized He had nurtured her, given her the idea, planted her in a good place, offered every opportunity to find the research and accomplish this work. But she was barren. "And I knew if I didn't put my hand to the work, the talent would wither," says Katherine.

While being stymied at her own inadequacies to paint what Christ experienced at the cross, she was like the Israelites going into Canaan. The whole camp was paralyzed with fear because of a report about the giants in the land, even though God had promised victory. They were looking at their inability to fight the giants and take the land. The Holy Spirit showed her that in the Spirit the painting was accomplished—it was her "Promised Land." But because of her fear she had avoided doing her part—to pick up the brush and paint!

She said, "OK, Lord, how do I begin?"

What she heard made sense to her as an artist: "Line upon line; just make a start and I'll be with you." God's grace pulled Katherine out of a tailspin. For the next six months she painted and completed the work, an eight-by-seven foot painting entitled *Tetelestar*, which means "paid in full." It hangs in Katherine's studio, and many people from various churches and states have come to see it. Although Katherine still considers it not quite complete—in the sense of ready to make prints of—she is grateful for the opportunity to be a vessel, to get to hold the brush and paint it.

An Offering

Katherine's art talent didn't emerge overnight. Although she had drawn and painted since childhood and studied art in college, she hadn't known the Giver of her talent. She grew up in a church, but never really heard that salvation needed to involve a personal relationship with Christ. At age twenty-five, however, she was diagnosed with pancreatic cancer. With a three-year-old son to consider and the three-month span the doctors had given her to live, she began to ask the hard questions: What happens after you die? How good do I have to be to get into heaven, if there really is a heaven?

"God," she cried out one day on the hill by their country house. "Are You really there? I don't know if You're real or if You're too big to care about what's happening to me, but I'm really scared. I need You to make yourself real to me in a way I can understand."

Although fireworks didn't go off that night, Katherine surrendered her life to Christ and was drawn to the Bible for the answers to her questions. "It was amazing; every question and fear I had, there was an answer for. It took me two weeks to understand that God was not just hearing but answering specifically what I had asked, and it dawned on me, God cares."

A tremendous peace came when Katherine realized that God loved her. She knew that if she died, she'd be with Him, and either way, He'd be with her. She still had a major health problem, a scared little three-year-old son, and a troubled marriage to handle, but she wasn't dealing with them alone. Feeling close to her own mortality, Katherine started doing nice things for everybody she loved.

Then one day several months later when she was at the grocery store, she called home and her husband said, "Your test results are back."

She leaned against the concrete wall by the pay phone for support and waited for the news.

"They're clear—you're OK."

At that point Katherine distinctly heard the Lord say, "I'm giving your life back; now use it to glorify Me."

Immediately after the good news, she came down with a severe case of pneumonia. As Katherine lay in the hospital for several weeks and then for months at home for recovery— through the fall, winter, and into the spring—she read the Bible constantly. The gratitude in her heart grew and grew.

"What can I do for You, Lord?" she kept asking. She wanted to give God something. The only thing she felt she could offer was her art talent. So although she'd always been restricted by a fear of failure, thinking she had to produce something wonderful, she gave Him her art talent.

In the hospital Katherine found a photo of a deer that she saved. Later she called the photographer and asked if she could do a pastel of it. After completing the pastel, she sold it to a catalog company. It went into publication and sold nationwide, eventually selling more than three million copies. The small royalty she received supported her and her children when her husband deserted them.

"I had been married for twelve years and was not skilled," Katherine says. "I had a $750 monthly house payment, utilities, and electric bills, and what I made at my job wouldn't stretch. But the deer covered it." Two other pastels Katherine drew went into print, providing needed income.

"It was just a sixty-cent piece of paper with colored dust (pastels) on it that God took, blessed, and multiplied," Katherine says. "God honored my prayer to further His kingdom. Because most of the salespeople were women trying to make extra income, the revenues went to support families, and to God's work if they tithed."

Katherine continues to paint in her studio and teaches art to children. Although she still battles a fear of failure, she doesn't let it derail the commissions the Lord brings her way.

She knows when we give God our talents and use them, His multiplication process is amazing!

When Your Dream Dies

"Even if you don't admit it, when you've always had the expectation that you'll be married and have children some-day," says Janis, "and the late thirties arrive and no relation-ship has turned into marriage, you can feel a sense of failure." The world gives you that message, and the church even rein-forces it.

You also can begin to put too much emphasis on succeeding in your job to make up for the lack of "marital success." She has found it is always important to separate who you are as a person from whether you have a "successful" job or the rela-tionships you've dreamed of.

In Janis's case, when she gave up the dream of marriage and experienced some disappointments in her job, it became easier to plod through day after day rather than setting new goals and dreaming a new dream—because she didn't want to risk failure. Ironically, a life-threatening illness is what shook her loose from the paralysis of fear. "I was depressed before I had cancer, and it created a stronger sense of purpose in life, not tied to succeeding in an endeavor or relationship. This pur-pose is tied to the way God wants me to live and to do the things He shows me," she says.

Following God often involves taking a risk, which is scary. Yet the risk results in being stretched and thus growing. The current adventure He's given Janis is to help start a brand-new church. "There's a chance it won't succeed or won't meet our expectations, but I've realized if I don't get out of my comfort zone to risk when God calls me to, I'll miss out on so much blessing.

"That's part of the excitement and uniqueness of being sin-gle," she adds. "I can take a risk when God calls me. I'm not tied down to a spouse's job or to children, so I can move to a different city or a new career if God directs me. I've moved four times alone, and there's *always* been blessing in it." To follow God and take the steps of faith He directs—that's success.

I love what Anthony Hopkins said recently: "It's the journey, not the arrival, that matters. The quest is always more important than the accomplishment."[1]

Afraid to Speak

Research shows that the fear of public speaking is the number one fear of Americans.[2] The fear of talking before an audience is greater than the fear of death, snakes, insects, and accidents! College surveys indicate that 80 to 90 percent of all students taking speech courses struggle with stage fright at the beginning of the course. Dale Carnegie stated that the statistics were even higher for adults: 100 percent of those taking his courses throughout the years were afraid of speaking in front of an audience.[3] So if you have ever been hesitant to get up and share your story with a group, you're not alone!

Even being a radio professional doesn't exempt a person from this anxiety. Liz Curtis Higgs spent ten years as a radio personality and never worried about speaking to thousands of listeners. "You can talk to 24,000 people at the same time and never get nervous," says Liz, "because you can't see them!"

Although she had the usual jitters about being on the air in the beginning, she discovered after her first month it was just like being on the phone. She loved it. Several years into her radio career Liz became a Christian and was asked by her church to give her testimony before more than five hundred people.

"What's a 'testimony'?" she asked her minister.

"They want to hear how you met Christ, what your life was like before and now that you are walking with God," he answered.

"You mean you want me to tell all these people that I was involved in the rock-and-roll, sex, and drugs lifestyle?" she asked him, nervous about what people would think of her. "I was afraid people wouldn't speak to me, they'd be so turned off to who I'd been before I knew Christ."

As the service approached, she was scared to death. "I couldn't eat for three days; and for me, that was traumatic. I never lose my appetite!" says Liz. By Wednesday night she was almost hyperventilating just thinking about getting up to the podium. She'd done theater as a child, but those are lines someone else wrote—not your personal story!

Her pastor leaned over and asked, "Are you going to be OK? You look terrible."

"No, but it's too late!" Liz said. He introduced her and she got up to walk to the microphone, knees shaking, mouth dry.

However, when Liz opened her mouth, a real spirit of calm settled down on her. *These are my friends*, she thought. *How could I be scared about speaking to them? I'll just tell them my story.*

Liz spoke for only four minutes; and the audience laughed, cried, and at the end stood up and clapped. She was shocked. Liz hadn't understood grace—that God had forgiven her and the people would too.

She floated off the lectern, overjoyed at being used by God. Her minister leaned over and whispered, "Liz, I believe you've found your calling."

People in the audience were from other churches, and several asked if she'd come and speak to their church. Within a year Liz was doing fifty presentations, and in a few years, she was speaking more than one hundred times a year. She has authored several books, with more in the works.

What can we learn from Liz's experience? Whatever talent you possess, when you find it, just do it! And don't let a little "anticipatory anxiety" hold you back. Like marathon runners who learn to move through the pain and keep running, learn to move through your jitters. A little bit of stage fright can have a positive effect, propelling you by raising your respiration and speeding up your heart. Even seasoned speakers and performers experience it. The result: You can think faster, talk more fluently—and with greater inspiration.[4]

And the more you speak, the more you'll enjoy it.

Overcoming Anxiety Little by Little

One of the best remedies for fears of any kind, even fear of failure, is what psychologists call "exposure": tackling the thing you've feared and avoided but doing it one step at a time. That's how Maggie came out of her prison of fear to reenter the adventure of life.

Maggie had gotten married right out of high school; within a year, she became pregnant with their first child and quit her job. After her son was born, she and the baby didn't go out at all unless her husband took her. With no car and no family or friends nearby, she had little reason to go out. And being shy and somewhat unsociable, Maggie really didn't mind.

But after months of being isolated, she wouldn't even open the front door to shake the mop for fear someone would see her. For the next five years Maggie didn't do anything unless her husband took her—grocery shopping included. If her husband took her out, she wasn't afraid, but by herself she was too fearful to venture out.

Fears Multiply

Maggie's experience shows that the only creative thing about fear is that it feeds on itself. When fear and worry cause us to avoid more and more situations, fear begins to dominate our lives. Fear robbed Maggie of joy, friendship, and even her freedom, just as though she were locked inside her home. She didn't like to go on vacations or anywhere, even for a weekend, afraid of being out of reach from home. During this time she developed heart problems and became afraid she might die at age twenty and leave a small baby.

"Many nights I went to bed thinking I was going to die and just knew I wouldn't wake up in the morning. With no family around, I feared what would happen to my child and husband if I died," she says. Although she took three or four kinds of medications for her heart problem, nothing really remedied the situation. Eventually the doctors found out her heart problems were from muscular deterioration from being sedentary and starving herself in an attempt to keep her weight down in her teenage years.

When Maggie accepted Christ and her husband began taking her to church, she began to want to go to a Bible study. Unfortunately, all of them were in the daytime when her husband was at work. It was hard to get a ride, so Maggie's desire for fellowship and study began to overtake her anxiety; she began to think about getting a driver's license. Her license had lapsed early in their marriage, and she hadn't driven for eight years.

Maggie took small steps and faced down her fears. Her husband got an old clunker for seventy-five dollars and taught her how to drive again. After weeks of practice, she got her license. Then she took her first adventure out.

"I was terrified even though my husband had shown me the way the night before," says Maggie. "I drove down a street where the speed limit was thirty miles per hour, but I couldn't even go fast enough to keep up with the traffic."

But once she started venturing out, she felt better about herself and inched out of her anxiety some more. "I came out of my fears little by little," says Maggie. She reentered life one step at a time—she didn't start by driving on the freeways the first week! At first she drove herself to the grocery store, church, or to women's houses for Bible study. Only recently has she driven by herself on the freeway.

For her next step, Maggie started exercising, first with walking and then doing aerobic exercises faithfully six days a week for an hour. Her husband and she also took up square dancing. As a result, her heart grew stronger and stronger. Maggie progressed to jogging outside by herself and now jogs long distances—an hour and a half each day.

Dealing with Setbacks

Maggie experienced setbacks; it wasn't an overnight trip out of fear into bold courage. One Fourth of July, she and her husband went to a fireworks show and were in the middle of a huge crowd of people. A joker set off tear gas; people feared it was poison gas, so mass hysteria broke out. Many people were trampled. Since then Maggie prefers being on the edge of a crowd instead of in the middle. But this obstacle didn't sideline her.

"I can't believe everything I do now and how much joy I have about it," Maggie says. "I'm now considering flying, which I've never done. I've always been terrified of flying, but that's my next frontier!"

❖

Oh, but man's reach
should exceed his grasp
or what's a heaven for?
—Robert Browning

❖

Bringing It Home

If you are afraid of trying something new you always wanted to tackle, like art lessons, writing a book, or jogging, don't let the fear of failure derail you. Begin to soar! Here are some ways to start taking small steps to freedom:

- List activities or circumstances you fear and usually avoid.

- Break one of them down into several smaller steps and list here.

_____

_____

_____

_____

_____

- Start doing the steps you've listed and meet the challenge—little by little!

- Share your dream or goal with someone. Sharing your idea or goal with a trusted friend helps bring it out of fantasy and into reality. Discuss how you're going to begin pursuing your passion.

- List some of your personal strengths: creative abilities, inner abilities, skills, intelligence for certain tasks, people skills, spiritual gifts, etc. Then pick one that you really want to pursue or develop and go for it, using the step-by-step method.

- Find some kind of exercise you could enjoy doing. Even if you just start with twenty minutes a day of walking and build up to more activity, you'll see benefits. Exercise is a tremendous stress and anxiety reducer and helps even the most severe anxiety disorders.

- Seek out people who are positive and believe in you. If there is just one person who believes in you and supports you, it can make all the difference. Everyone needs a support system—to be around people who build up instead of criticize and tear down, especially when embarking on a new direction.

Lifesavers and Worrybusters

God has given each of you some special abilities; be sure to use them to help each other, passing on to others God's many kinds of blessings. Are you called to preach? Then preach as though God himself were speaking through you. Are you called to help others? Do it with all the strength and energy that God supplies, so that God will be glorified through Jesus Christ—to him be glory and power forever and ever. (1 Pet. 4:10–11, TLB)

Why is it that he gives us these special abilities to do certain things best? It is that God's people will be equipped to do better work for him, building up the Church, the body of Christ, to a position of strength and maturity; until finally we all believe alike about our salvation and about our Savior, God's Son, and all become full-grown in the Lord—yes, to the point of being filled full with Christ. (Eph. 4:12–13, TLB)

It is the same and only Holy Spirit who gives all these gifts and powers, deciding which each one of us should have. (1 Cor. 12:11, TLB)

Such confidence as this is ours through Christ before God. Not that we are competent in ourselves to claim anything for ourselves, but our competence comes from God. (2 Cor. 3:4–5)

He has showered down upon us the richness of his grace—for how well he understands us and knows what is best for us at all times. (Eph. 1:8, TLB)

I can do everything God asks me to with the help of Christ who gives me the strength and power. (Phil. 4:13, TLB)

He who fills me with His dynamic power has made me able to cope with any situation. (Phil. 4:13, Barclay)

Each time he said, "No, but I am with you; that is all you need. My power shows up best in weak people." Now I am glad to boast about how weak I am; I am glad to be a living demonstration of Christ's power, instead of showing off my own power and abilities. (2 Cor. 12:9, TLB)

For I know the plans I have for you, says the Lord. They are plans for good and not for evil, to give you a future and a hope. In those days when you pray, I will listen. You will find me when you seek me, if you look for me in earnest.
(Jer. 29:11–13, TLB)

Do not let this Book of the Law depart from your mouth; meditate on it day and night, so that you may be careful to do everything written in it. Then you will be prosperous and successful. (Josh. 1:8, NIV)

Work hard and cheerfully at all you do, just as though you were working for the Lord. (Col. 3:23, TLB)

9

When the Worst Happens: Overcoming Fear of the Uncontrollable

Have no fear of sudden disaster or of the ruin that overtakes the wicked, for the LORD will be your confidence and will keep your foot from being snared.
—PROVERBS 3:25–26

The headlines of the past year are full of disasters and calamities: powerful earthquake hits California; massive hurricane batters Florida; fire destroys Chicago neighborhood; family of six killed by drunk driver. Even in the heartland of America, my own city, we were touched by disaster: the bombing of the Federal Building in Oklahoma City, April 19, 1995. It killed 168 people, 19 of them innocent children in the America's Kids Day Care Center, wounded hundreds, left 30 children orphaned and 219 with only one parent. We live in a violent world, and anxiety about disasters is on the rise—fear about those uncontrollable events that crash into our lives and change things forever.

"I can handle the day-to-day struggles like sickness and financial problems, my husband not paying child support, or losing the house," a woman said recently. "But I couldn't handle a major disaster like that bombing in your city. I don't know if my faith could stand that kind of test, and I don't know if I could survive the tragedy if one of my kids had been in it."

Many storms in life are uncontrollable, says Larry Jones of Feed the Children Ministry. Larry has seen some of the worst disasters in the twentieth century: the famine in Ethiopia, the war in Bosnia, the torrential floods of the Midwest, Hurricane Gilbert that destroyed much of the island of Jamaica. And Larry's ministry has been there to deliver help.

"Stormy marriages, financial storms, physical storms like cancer, stormy plagues like AIDS—we can't always avoid or prevent them," he says. "But we can control the way we respond to them. If we control our reaction, we can tap into God's provision and ride out the storm in peace."[1]

But what about when the uncontrollable comes crashing into *our* lives unexpectedly? Is God able to sustain us?

Tragedy Hits

Cyndi and Steve were the happy parents of two sons, ages ten and six, awaiting the birth of their first daughter when tragedy struck their lives in December of 1991. Steve and Cyndi were committed Christians, and Steve was on his way to Sunday School one morning when he was hit head-on by a drunk driver. He was taken to Mercy Health Center with a severe brain injury and not expected to live past twenty-four hours. However, in less than two months, both Steve and Cyndi would be patients at Mercy—Cyndi giving birth, while her husband struggled to live.

For five months, Steve lay in a coma. He saw nothing, heard nothing, and did nothing. Repeatedly the neurosurgeon said, "I see no significant change."

Normally Cyndi wasn't a worrier. "I could get stressed-out over grades when I was in college, but temperamentally, I'm laid-back," she says. With her husband in a life-threatening condition, the doctors only giving him a fair chance to make it, and huge, mounting medical bills for critical care, she was filled with anxiety about some big, very real issues:

• Will my husband ever recover?

- How am I going to have this baby by myself, without Steve?

- How can I go through delivery alone?

- Am I going to have to put this newborn in daycare and go to work?

- How are we going to make it financially?

Cyndi and her family's experience is a good example of the principle that 98 percent of what we worry about doesn't come true. The other 2 percent comes true, and we can't control it anyway.

Her first challenges were single-parenting and being at the hospital all she could while in the last stage of pregnancy. One day she got a devastating report that Steve's condition was deteriorating and he could be in the coma indefinitely. A visiting pastor told her, "We don't always get a miracle." That was one of her darkest nights. She couldn't sleep and knew she could easily be lost in a pit of fear and worry.

Choosing to Believe

As Cyndi walked up and down the stairs at Mercy Hospital the next day, words from Jeremiah 29:11 went through her mind: "'For I know the plans that I have for you,' declares the LORD, 'plans to prosper you and not to harm you, plans to give you hope and a future.'" That verse kept flashing on the screen of her mind.

"You believed this before the accident, and you've stood on that truth for minor circumstances. It's still true now," God seemed to say to her, encouraging her to believe, regardless of what the circumstances looked like before or after the head-on injury. "Do you *believe* I am who I say I am?"

Cyndi chose to believe and persisted each day no matter how things looked on the outside. "Regardless of where we end up, I was convinced that Scripture is still true that there is a future for me and my family and good for our lives ahead," Cyndi says. Holding onto that truth helped her keep up her hope and stay out of the pit of anxiety. From then on, she didn't struggle with feeling abandoned or bitter. But she did have some real worries about the upcoming birth and finances. She faced many daily struggles—one of the big ones being how she was going to raise her boys without a father.

On February 14, six weeks after the accident, Steve lay in a coma, and Cyndi was eight months pregnant. She walked out on their deck and found Tate, their six-year-old, hugging some photos of nude women. He'd found a stash of hard-core pornography in a plastic bag down in the creek behind their house and had spread it out all over the deck to look at it. "Mom, isn't she beautiful?" Tate said, his eyes shining.

Cyndi was mortified. Her six-year-old son's innocence was robbed, and there was no dad to handle this. She sat down and sobbed, "I can't deal with this." Her first thought was to call a friend her age who had children a little older. She advised that Cyndi ask Jeremy, her ten-year-old, about the pornography. They had a talk about it, and Jeremy told her he and a friend had found it, looked at it, and put it back in the plastic bag in the creek. Cyndi began to see that in Tate's openness, God was exposing the pornography so she could address the issue with both of her sons. At the end of that day she thought, *Look how God is bringing help. I am not alone.*

Just a few weeks later she was faced with her next worry: how she would deliver their baby alone. Steve had been a great labor coach and support, and she couldn't imagine delivery without him.

But Katelyn was delivered in a warm family atmosphere with twenty-five friends and family in the waiting room, cheering her on and celebrating. A great woman OB-Gyn and three friends served as terrific labor coaches. In fact, they made the best labor and delivery team she could have hoped for. She was definitely *not alone!*

"Katelyn was a beautiful, healthy, blond, curly-haired baby who looked just like a cherub," Cyndi says. She was an easy, happy infant who slept all night and was almost angelic her first year—which was truly God's gift. But now Cyndi would have to face her fear of having to put her in daycare.

"Initially I wasn't worried about finances," she says. She was just making it from day to day focusing on Steve's survival and cushioned from other concerns. But when Steve emerged from the coma five months after the accident, Cyndi was faced with a new bundle of worries. One of these hit her the day she was being shown the rehabilitation unit that Steve would be put into for an indefinite number of months. All of a sudden, the bleakness and severity of what they were facing hit home.

"Here's where we'll show him how to open a can, so that eventually when he's at home alone while you're working he can fix something to eat," the social worker said.

God's Provision

Upon hearing their fate, Cyndi sat down at the table and wept. She didn't know how she could put her baby in daycare and support the family. But in actuality, this fear never materialized. In March a former client of Steve's had a fundraiser and in one day raised $7,000. The Radio Council held an auction and made $17,000. Their church started a fund that went on for three and a half years, and people contributed thousands of dollars to their family's support. "Katelyn never had to go to daycare because the church took care of us," says Cyndi. "It was a great lesson to me on not borrowing worry from the future."

Cyndi's situation was like that of the widow whom God helped in the midst of famine. The widow had only enough meal and oil left for one loaf and was gathering sticks for a fire to cook her and her son's last meal.

Elijah asked her for bread, and after she explained her situation, he said: "Don't be afraid. Go home and do as you have said. But first make a small cake of bread for me from what you have and bring it to me, and then make something for yourself and your son. For this is what the LORD, the God of Israel, says: 'The jar of flour will not be used up and the jug of oil will not run dry until the day the LORD gives rain on the land'"(1 Kings 17:13–14).

She went away and did as Elijah had told her. And sure enough, her family had food enough for a long time. She never ran out of oil or flour until the famine ended. In a similar way, the funds raised for the Lamb family lasted until the settlement from the insurance company was finalized. After Steve's being hospitalized for twenty-two months and unable to earn an income, they are debt free.

And though her husband is now uninsurable and in a wheelchair, unable to ever work a full-time job, Cyndi doesn't worry about how they are going to make it financially. God has been too faithful for her to fall into fear. The God who spoke to her on the stairs of the hospital, "I still have a future and a hope for you," is the same God who carries them today. Steve has started a ministry to children of divorced parents and is pursuing writing. His attitude is refreshing.

"Although I may look broken—damaged—on the outside, don't let this wheelchair fool you," says Steve. "I have been healed. Prayers have been answered in many ways: the fact that I survived at all and came out of the coma with all my long-term memory, sense of humor, and creative abilities still intact.

"But the greatest healing of all has been in my spirit. I do not struggle with anger or bitterness. I do not blame God or harbor deep resentment against the guy who hit me. I know we live in a fallen world, and terrible things happen to all of us—just ask Jesus."

Lots of days are difficult and complicated. But most of all, Steve has learned to savor each day and is thankful for the new life he's been given. "Not the kind of life that is handed to you wrapped in paper with a bow on top, but new life that is a process. It's been long and painful, but then birth always is. So is rebirth," says Steve.

⊷≡◉⊂≡⊷

Put your powerlessness in God's almighty power,
and find in waiting on God your deliverance.
—Andrew Murray

⊷≡◉⊂≡⊷

Look from the Top

Do you ever feel like you're on the bottom or overwhelmed by circumstances—not "on top of things" like you'd like to be? If so, you're not alone! But God has a remedy. If you get caught in the crush of life and pushed down, says Amy Carmichael in one of my favorite entries in her devotional *Edges of His Ways*,

> The next thing we know is that we are groveling in the dust. Things are on the top of *us*; we are not on the top of anything. So God calls us, "Look from the top" (Song of Songs 4:8). "Come with Me from all that, come up the mountain with Me, and look from the top." In everyday life this simply means look from everything up to the Lord Jesus, Who is our Peace, our Victory, and our Joy, for we are where we look. From below, things feel impossible, people seem impossible (some people at least), and we ourselves feel most impossible of all. From the top we see as our Lord sees; He sees not what is only, but what shall be. He is not discouraged, and as we look with Him, our discouragement vanishes, and we can sing a new song."[2]

Bringing It Home

When you feel anxious or worried about people and things that seem impossible, ask God to let you look from the top, as Amy Carmichael suggests, so you can see things, even if for a moment, from *His* point of view. It will make a big difference!

Get anchored in God's love for you. Pray every day, "God, teach me that You love me." What helped Cyndi more than anything else in the crisis she faced was that before going into it, she had a deep belief that God loved her. That foundation didn't come easily; in fact, as a young Christian she struggled with believing God loved her because she came from a divorced family with a faithless, alcoholic father who could never be depended on. But a youth leader who knew her struggle encouraged her to pray *every single day*, "Lord, teach me that You love me." Throughout her twenties and early thirties Cyndi continued praying that prayer each day and found herself consistently discovering how much He loved her. As a result, God's love became a real anchor in her life. That's a prayer He loves to answer! And believing in His love for you is an undergirding truth that, if you internalize not only in your head but also in your heart, will help you face any difficulty or crisis with more faith and less anxiety.

You must really know in your gut that whatever happens, God loves you and has your family's best interests at heart, and ultimately He has a plan that *He will see accomplished*—a plan for "a future filled with hope" (Jer. 29:11, *The Promise*). Armed with this belief, Cyndi didn't waste her energy fighting God or the circumstances or being angry at Him. "The *why's* came to visit, but they never took up residence," she adds with a chuckle.

If you constantly struggle with knowing God loves you and can't identify with Cyndi's belief in God's care and love, you can still pray this even in the darkest moment: "I want to believe that You love me, and I want to believe Your Word. Would you show me and *teach me Your love?*"

Get your own "big picture" perspective on life's difficulties. I've found this helps us cope both with the daily stresses *or* the big crises; it is a great prevention for panic. In our early years of marriage we would get one set of problems solved—we'd get the kids well, the bills paid, and hope that around the bend there wouldn't be any more problems—and then another wave of problems would hit us. SLAP!—just like a big ocean wave knocking me down when I least expected it, I'd be caught off guard. Anxiety would rise as I thought, *Oh, no! Another problem!* I cringed whenever I read in John 15 about pruning; I read around the passages on suffering and trials.

Here's a thought that helped me: "Life is difficult. . . . This is a great truth, one of the greatest truths . . . because once we truly see this truth, we truly transcend it. Once we truly know that life is difficult—once we truly understand and accept it— then life is no longer difficult. Because once it has been accepted, the fact that life is difficult no longer matters."[3]

As Steve and Cyndi found, bad things happen to everyone. Just ask Jesus. He came into the painful world we live in and wasn't spared problems. Steve and Cyndi conclude: "We think life is supposed to be a smooth road with little pockets of interruptions, trials, and change. But the truth is life is a road full of change and difficulties with little pockets of serenity." And part of why Christians are here, they believe, is to show the world how to solve problems, even seemingly insurmountable ones, *with Christ*. And that big perspective has helped them courageously cope and even celebrate in the midst of some very difficult times.

―━◉━―

Be assured, if you walk with Him
and look to Him
and expect help from Him,
He will never fail you.
—George Mueller

―━◉━―

The Wonder of God's Presence in Crisis

Part of the wonder is how God can use even the worst of situations the enemy meant for destruction and evil and *transform* them and us! He can turn blizzards into blessings, trials into trust-builders, and even calamities into comfort. With His awesome presence and His power in the midst of our crisis, He actually *delivers us* from fear so that we emerge as whole, healthy individuals.

When Priscilla Salyers pushed the door open to her office at the U.S. Customs office on the fifth floor of the Murrah Federal Building the morning of April 19, 1995, she had no idea that her life and the lives of her coworkers and friends would be changed forever. After picking up the mail on the first floor earlier than she had in seven years and visiting with her friend Paul Ice over coffee, Priscilla went to her desk to begin work.

Moments later, as she picked up the phone, a blast like a huge sonic boom shook the building, and suddenly everything went black. Priscilla was picked up by a huge whirlwind. Flashes of light like stars swirled around her. Wind roared in her ears, and she lost control of her body.

Trapped!

When everything stopped, she felt a massive jolt and realized that she couldn't move anything except her left arm. What Priscilla didn't know is that a huge truck bomb had destroyed the Federal Building, and she had fallen from the fifth floor to below the first floor, which was later called "The Pit." She was trapped face down under concrete and rubble.

As the heaviness of silence sunk in, Priscilla prayed two things: "Lord, keep me calm and give me the wisdom for survival." Over and over as she prayed those words, she began to remember how earthquake victims who survived had made it three days—because they found an air pocket to breathe. With her left hand, she dug out some rubble from under her neck to create an air pocket. Only then could she breathe, but it took every ounce of strength and concentration she had.

Finally rescuers found her, and a man closed his hand over hers. All her worries transferred to his hand—it was like God's hand extended to her. Such peace and safety she felt! But that respite was short-lived, for soon the man said, "Priscilla, we have to leave."

Panic swept through her; she gripped his hand tighter, begging him not to go, "Please don't leave me! Don't leave me . . ."

What she didn't know until later was that a second bomb threat caused a forced evacuation of the entire building. The second silence was worse than the first. For four hours she lay there—sometimes hyperventilating, several times desperately wanting to fall asleep, and at times furious at the men who hadn't come back to rescue her.

After what seemed an eternity, Priscilla could hear movement and voices in the distance. She pounded on the surface next to her so they wouldn't miss her. Then she heard a voice say, "We've got a live one down here," as someone took her hand. That same comforting, peaceful feeling she'd had before filled her.

The Rescue

Rescuers worked with chainsaws and the "Jaws of Life" to lift the concrete and rubble off of Priscilla. First, pressure was released from her head, and then her right arm, left leg, and right leg were freed. All of a sudden, Priscilla was flipped over onto a spinal board. Pain shot through her body; she moaned and gasped for every breath.

But then she saw her first sight in hours—the blue sky above. To her left it looked like a war zone, and she knew then the entire building was devastated. The next thing she knew she was being passed from one rescuer to another out of the building. Face after face smiled and encouraged her: "You'll make it," they said, as paramedics put her in an ambulance and sped to the hospital.

After five days in the hospital, where her broken ribs, collapsed lung, and other injuries were treated, Priscilla came home to an emotional welcome from her husband, two sons, family, and friends. In the midst of pain, she was preoccupied with two questions: (1) God, what do You expect of me now—how can I put my life back together? (2) I've heard so many people say, "We were praying for you, and you made it," and yet a lot of people were praying for Mickey and Paul and the others who were Christians and yet died. Why, God?

Sitting up in a recliner that first night after everyone had gone to bed, Priscilla opened the Bible and read Romans 12. Present your body to God, the passage said. Whatever gifts you have, use them for others and do it well; really love people and even invite them home for dinner. Don't repay evil for evil (she knew then God would take care of those who bombed the building; she didn't have to hold bitterness against them). She saw clearly that God was not expecting her to do fantastic works, but if she lived the way He described here, then the reason she survived would be fulfilled.

He Rescued Them

The next day was her good friend Mickey Maroney's memorial service, and she was determined to go, even in a wheelchair. They had worked together for six and a half years in Secret Service, and she knew how devoted he was to Christ. She was really struggling and asking, "Why, God? Why didn't he make it?"

The passage read at Mickey's service was Psalm 34:6–7: "This poor man cried and the LORD heard him, and saved him out of all his troubles. The angel of the LORD encamps around those who fear Him, and rescues them" (NASB). She was thinking, *Why didn't God rescue Mickey and Paul and the others?* And then it hit her—*He did rescue them. He took them home!*

Then her mind flashed back to how He'd been with her: Jesus was present with her in the bombed building when she was buried under concrete. When the rescuer held her hand, it was like Jesus' hand. His Spirit reminded her to breathe slowly and keep calm so she could get air in the small space. Wherever Priscilla was, Jesus was *with her.*

Jesus' presence surrounded her in the hospital and in the outpouring of comfort from friends and people all over the country, many she didn't even know. And she knew God was also with those who died, sending angels to care for them and take them to heaven. She knew He would be with her in the long recovery that lay ahead and that He had a purpose for the rest of her life.

His nearness to her in the face of death was so real that Priscilla doesn't fear death anymore. His peace is so overwhelming that she knows when it's time for her to join Paul, Claude, and her other friends who died, she won't fear, *for Jesus will be with her.*

This knowledge and peace has sustained Priscilla during months of pain and grieving and has brought her into more freedom than she's ever known. Before the bombing, she was very timid and never spoke before a group, even a small one. But a few weeks after the tragedy, a church service was held for paramedics who were struggling with guilt about not saving more people than they did.

"I knew there was something I needed to share with those paramedics," Priscilla says. "But at first I thought, *not me*. All my life I was too scared to get up in front of a group."

A friend had been encouraging her for a long time to go back to church, but since her husband didn't attend, she'd gotten out of the habit. "You could really help people. You have such a great testimony," he'd said.

So Priscilla attended the service and prayed, "Lord, give me the words." That night as she faced more than seventy-five rescuers, she told them about the incredible peace she had when the fireman was holding her hand. And she said that to every person they touched, they gave a priceless gift—they were God's hand extended to them in either their last moments or until they were rescued.

Before, Priscilla was too shy to share Christ, but not anymore. She is no longer ashamed to let anybody know that God brought her through and to share the good news about Christ.

When she has shared her story at churches, people have come up and cried as one woman did, "I really needed to hear what you shared."

"If I can touch even one person," Priscilla says, "if what I learned through this experience helps other people, then there's a purpose. And when I get down, I have to focus back on that—God brought me through for a reason."

Bringing It Home

How to Overcome Tragedy

Ask God to help you sense His presence in your life, especially in the storms. God's promise is that *He will be with us*. From the time that we become His children through believing in Jesus Christ, His presence indwells us, and His care for us is secure, just as it was for Priscilla. God doesn't break His promises. "For God Himself has said, I will not in any way fail you nor give you up nor leave you without support. I will not. I will not, I will not in any degree leave you helpless, nor forsake nor let you down [relax My hold on you].—Assuredly not!" (Heb. 13:5, AMP).

But although God is with us, we often don't sense His presence or realize He's there. Just as the disciples didn't recognize Jesus when He came to them on the water in the midst of the storm, when we're in a dark place we may feel He hasn't shown up. When that happens and you feel left alone, pray that God will open your eyes and heart to see what He's doing and to know the truth—that He's with you.

Next, personalize God's promises for protection as you speak them aloud:

You are my hiding place!
You protect me from trouble,
and You put songs in my heart
because You have saved me.
(Ps. 32:7, *The Promise*)

The LORD will protect you
and keep you safe from all dangers.
The LORD will protect you
now and always wherever you go.
(Ps. 121:7–8, *The Promise*)

Live under the protection of God Most High
and stay in the shadow of God All-Powerful.
Then you will say to the LORD,
"You are my fortress, my place of safety;
you are my God, and I trust You."
(Ps. 91:1–2, *The Promise*)

The LORD is my light and my salvation—whom shall I fear? The LORD is the stronghold of my life—of whom shall I be afraid? (Ps. 27:1)

I have set the LORD always before me; because he is at my right hand, I will not be shaken. Therefore my heart is glad and my tongue rejoices. (Ps. 16:8–9)

God is our refuge and strength, an ever present help in trouble. Therefore we will not fear, though the earth give way and

though the mountains f...
waters roar ar⌐ ⌐
ing. (Ps. 46:1–.

I may walk throu
but I won't be afra   ...c,
and your shepherd   ..es me feel safe.
(Ps. 23:4, *The Promi..)*

The Proverbs are also full of promises and assurances of God's protection: Proverbs 1:33; 3:23; 21:31; and 18:10 to name just a few. And just think: His promises are backed by all the honor of His name (see Ps. 138:2). Speaking words of truth that God is our Protector dispels fear wherever we are— in a storm, a bombing, on an airplane, or a highway—and reminds us that our safety is in the Lord.

Be aware that God is our true environment and dwelling place, and we're surrounded by His care each moment of the day. Wherever we are and whatever may happen, He is with us and within us! The Christian is guarded on all sides by the Lord. We have God before us (Isa. 48:17), God behind us (Isa. 30:21), God on our right (Ps. 16:8), God to our left (Job 23:8–9), God above us (Ps. 36:7), God's arms underneath us (Deut. 33:27), and His spirit within us (1 Cor. 6:19).[4]

If you are afraid, serve someone else. One of the ways Priscilla has found healing is to reach out to others—from the first group of paramedics she shared with to other people in churches in need of hope and inspiration. She reached out to the grieving families of Paul and Claude, her closest coworkers, and every other week gets together with a small group of survivors for dinner. They have all lost friends, family, or coworkers and are all dealing with pain. They laugh about happy memories and cry together when they miss their friends. But being together, talking, and helping each other aids the healing process. Becoming isolated and preoccupied with self only increases fear and anxiety.

"There is no greater cure for our personal fears than to help others in need," says Don Gossett. "Victorious saints of

God are persons who, though human and prone to fear, spend
themselves in service and thus have no time for worry."[5]

Find someone to encourage and help—a single parent who
needs assistance, a child in need of support, an elderly person
who is a shut-in due to ill health. Don't wait until your problems are solved to help someone else! When you share God's
love by serving others, you'll experience His peace.

Lifesavers and Worrybusters

Now the Lord who created you . . . says, Don't be afraid, for I
have ransomed you; I have called you by name; you are mine.
When you go through deep waters and great trouble, I will be
with you. When you go through rivers of difficulty, you will
not drown! When you walk through the fire of oppression, you
will not be burned up—the flames will not consume you. For I
am the Lord your God, your Savior, the Holy One of
Israel. . . . You are precious to me and honored, and I love you.
Don't be afraid, for I am with you. (Isa. 43:1–5, TLB)

The angel of the LORD encamps
   around those who fear him,
   and he delivers them. (Ps. 34:7)

Have mercy on me, O God, have mercy on me,
   for in you my soul takes refuge.
I will take refuge in the shadow of your wings
   until the disaster has passed. (Ps. 57:1)

For I know the thoughts and plans that I have for you, says the
Lord, thoughts and plans for welfare and peace and not for
evil, to give you hope in your final outcome. (Jer. 29:11, AMP)

He will have no fear of bad news;
his heart is steadfast, trusting in the LORD.
(Ps. 112:7)

He [Jesus] replied, "You of little faith, why are you so afraid?"
Then he got up and rebuked the winds and the waves, and it
was completely calm. (Matt. 8:26)

You will not fear the terror of night,
nor the arrow that flies by day. (Ps. 91:5)

For I am the LORD, your God,
　who takes hold of your right hand
and says to you, Do not fear;
　I will help you. (Isa. 41:13)

10

Either Way You Win: Overcoming Fears about Health Problems

Everything can be taken away from a person but the freedom to choose how to react to any given set of circumstances.
—Victor Frankl

On a June afternoon in 1991, Nancy, a forty-year-old wife and mother of two sons, was diagnosed with breast cancer. On that day, the "Big C" quickly swept in to take over her life, with its accompanying surgery, anxiety, hair loss, and pain. Because the cancer had spread into the bone of her neck and was at Stage 4, in a matter of five days she had a mastectomy and breast reconstruction surgery. She also began an aggressive round of chemotherapy that would last for fourteen months and radiation treatments that would take four months.

But in the time of dealing with the "Big C" of cancer, the Lord ministered to Nancy and became her "Bigger C"—her Comforter, Constant Companion, Counselor, and even Conqueror. While the doctor didn't give her the statistics at first, he later sat down and told her in the stage and type of cancer she had, there was only a 10 to 20 percent cure rate, and her chances for recovery were very slim.

The Fight of Faith

To Focus on God

The day Nancy heard the diagnosis from her doctor and was told she must see a surgeon immediately, she drove home and thought, *I can't cry yet; I might have a wreck. I'll wait until I get in the house to cry.* Then on the way into the house, she saw the mail, and one of the top letters was from a ministry. The envelope said, "You can live above your circumstances."

When she opened it, the first thing she saw was a sketch of Daniel in the lion's den. Daniel was looking up, and the lions were below him. Second Chronicles 20:12 was written below: "Fix your eyes on Jesus no matter what your circumstances!"

Nancy got out her Bible and read the story of Daniel and then turned to 2 Chronicles 20 to read the story of Jehoshaphat. As she poured over the words, the whole chapter seemed to speak to right where she was. "The part about 'We were powerless and don't know what to do' was the key," says Nancy. She spoke honestly to God: "OK, Lord, I'm powerless against this cancer and don't know what to do, but I'm determined to fix myself on You."

That attitude and determination—*to fix her focus on God* instead of the circumstances and disease of cancer—was the difference between life and death, between anxiety and peace for Nancy. She did finally sit down and have a good cry, but it wasn't in utter hopelessness.

"I grieved when I considered the surgery and all the treatment I'd be facing, but I had hope," says Nancy. "A couple of verses down in the chapter it says, 'Go out and face the enemy and you will see the salvation of the Lord.'" *OK*, she thought, *they didn't run either. Instead they prayed and sent out the praisers ahead, and the Lord sent ambush against the enemy.* So Nancy determined to face her enemy—cancer—and do everything she had to do and to fix her eyes on God and get the eternal instead of the internal perspective.

Several times Nancy had dreams about dying and dealt with her share of fear and worry. One of her greatest fears was that she'd be "out of it" or lose function or the ability to speak and control herself. But six months after her last treatment in January 1993, she got the first bone scan that showed she was completely healed. And every six months to a year she has more CT scans, but she has recovered her health and remains free of cancer. Here are some things she learned in this long battle against cancer with God as her Comforter, Constant Companion, Counselor, and Conqueror, principles that apply to facing any health problem:

Don't assume it's an automatic death sentence if you are diagnosed with breast cancer or other serious illness. Whenever there is a medical problem or negative diagnosis, see it as a possibility, but see God as the final authority. If your mom or grandmother suffered with cancer years ago, remember that great strides in treatment have been made.

When there was a diagnosis or new information, Nancy held it up to the light of Scripture. She found comfort in looking up specific verses in the Bible that addressed the problem. For example, when the doctors told her that the medications and chemotherapy could adversely affect her heart, she looked up many Scriptures on the heart and meditated on them, such as, "A cheerful heart is good medicine" (Prov. 17:22) and, "Comfort and strengthen your hearts in every good work and word" (2 Thess. 2:17, NASB). "Find a Scripture you can call your own, to remind you that God knows your problem and will work in your situation," she adds.

Don't isolate yourself; you'll get even more afraid if you're alone. Nancy and her husband had just started going to a new church in Austin, Texas, where they had recently moved. They didn't know people at the church, and it would have been easy to stay at home. But Nancy found out there was a Tuesday morning ladies Bible study and went to it. There she got to know many ladies who prayed with her, cried with her when the chemotherapy was causing depression and other side effects, and rejoiced with her when she had a good report. They encouraged her without being preachy or giving pat answers, which was a big help. Also, her husband was supportive, and their youngest son, who was in his senior year of high school, offered his encouragement and love.

Don't be afraid to call friends to pray with you when you're having a rough day. She had a few friends who said, "Nancy, call me and just say, 'Pray for me; I'm going through a tough time.' You don't even need to tell me what's happening!" Don't be afraid to reach out to people on the telephone, at church, or in support groups.

⟶═◉═⟵

Faith is for that which lies on the other side of reason. Faith is what makes life bearable, with all of its tragedies and ambiguities and sudden, startling joys.
—Madeline L'Engle

⟶═◉═⟵

Know that God meets each of us individually. He will walk through everything with you. He will give you what you need at the time you need the grace! During one of her months of treatment, Nancy attended a workshop to learn how to lead small support groups. There she met an older man whose wife had recently died of cancer. He shared with special compassion: "Either way, Nancy, you win. If you get well and recover from cancer, you win. If you die, you win because you get to be with Jesus."

When he had to leave a little early, he smiled at her and said, "Remember, Nancy, either way you win!" God brought people like this across her path regularly to encourage her.

Remember, it's God who carries you. You can rest in Him and not have to do all the work yourself! During the time of surgery and chemotherapy treatment, Nancy felt like she was almost in a bubble because God was carrying her. But after she had recovered a little, she felt like, "Now I've got to fight the battle of faith and conquer these mental struggles so I can stand strong and help others." She was determined not to be preoccupied with her own health problems.

While "standing strong" on her own she got weary, and God brought a reminder to her that she could depend on Him. She was down in the dumps after the doctor had given her the bleak statistics of how small her chances of long-term survival were. At the same time, her brother-in-law was dying with cancer, and watching him die was difficult. Her fears multiplied.

That Sunday morning in church a couple introduced the special music they were going to sing with the verse Philippians 1:6: "For I am confident of this very thing, that He who has begun a good work in you will perfect [complete] it until the day of Christ Jesus" (NASB). As they began to sing the words to that Scripture, tears rolled down Nancy's cheeks, and she remembered, *God's not through with me yet. He's going to complete what He started.* Just hearing this verse lifted her out of the dumps of depression and filled her with hope.

Through the song, God was gently saying, "You don't have to do all the work yourself; I'm here with you." He was faithful to bring the words she needed on many occasions through a call from a friend, a song, or a Scripture.

Music can minister to you in special ways even when you don't have the energy to read the Bible or talk with someone. Sometimes after treatment Nancy would lie in bed for hours so lethargic she couldn't do anything. Her husband would play a cassette of the Psalms on tape with a music background or Scripture praise music. "I would listen when I could do nothing else," said Nancy. "It absorbed in my spirit and helped me focus on Christ and experience His presence."

A year ago, Nancy was struck by the verses in 2 Corinthians 1:3–4 that say, "Praise be to the God and Father of our Lord Jesus Christ, the Father of compassion and the God of all comfort, who comforts us in all our troubles, so that we can comfort those in any trouble with the comfort we ourselves have received from God." She realized she had a great desire to comfort and encourage other women who struggled with cancer.

Only a few days later, she had another series of CT scans, and the first one showed that she had a bowel obstruction.

Anxiety threatened her peace: *Could it be the cancer has recurred? What if I have to have surgery again?* But she resisted the fear and thought: *No, I'm not going to die. I'm going to strengthen and encourage others, and I can't if I'm dead.* As it turned out, there was no bowel obstruction or sign of new cancer growth.

However, the experience did make her reflect on the meaning of "victory" and her role in encouraging others. "Right now I'm healthy and in remission. But whether I'm cancer-free or not, my purpose is to be a comfort to others," Nancy says. "The victory is not just being cancer-free. I could think, *What if I start doing seminars then the cancer comes back—would it ruin my testimony?* No, it wouldn't because my testimony is that God is faithful and He's there with us, and I do have the victory no matter what."

What Nancy has learned is that we pray for healing and appropriate all the grace and truth God provides in Scripture; we employ all the resources medical science has and do our part to care for our bodies. But the final outcome is with God, whether our healing is on this side or in the ultimate healing of heaven.

The challenge, the choice, and the fight of faith for Nancy remains—to keep her eyes on Jesus. "When I do, I'm not afraid of the future or health problems because I know He'll be with me and give me whatever I need to get through it." He's walked her through a long wilderness to victory on the other side. Now Nancy is using the health she has, is grateful for each day of life, and has written a devotional book especially for cancer patients.

-+≈◉═+-

When God allows extraordinary trials,
he gives extraordinary comfort.
—Anonymous

-+≈◉═+-

Don't Waste Your Troubles

Lisbeth Alexander uses 2 Corinthians 1:3–4 to say that everything she went through in her double mastectomy and chemotherapy ten years ago would have been wasted if she hadn't used her experience to reach out and share help with others. She kept a Gratefulness Journal, and every day she wrote down things that people did that helped her: a verse she was given, flowers that arrived, even the small pillow her mother brought when she was experiencing pain under her arm after surgery. She listed the special hat someone brought her, which was much more attractive than a turban for "after chemo." Later she had her dressmaker make similar hats, which she gives to cancer friends.

"We tend to forget the little things," says Lisbeth. "But all through the Scriptures it says, 'Remember what God did!'" Remembering the kindness and comfort she received has helped her pass out buckets of comfort to others. Since her recovery, Lisbeth has reached out to more than 125 women with cancer. She not only keeps a list of their names and addresses in her Daytimer so she can send them cards at Christmas and other times; she also helps in these creative ways:

Give a blank book and make a Gratefulness Journal. Lisbeth keeps blank journals on hand and takes one when she visits someone diagnosed with cancer. She encourages them to write in it every day, starting with a simple list of helps: the phone call that came at just the right time when you were feeling down; the card your son sent you; the Scripture that lifted your heart. On the days that are really rough, you can look in the journal and see how God has worked. Keeping your journal will also enable you to remember what helped you so you can pass on the act of kindness to someone else when they need it.

Start or join a support group. Lisbeth is part of a "Bosom Buddies" group that meets for lunch once a month. They chat, laugh, and share things that have worked in their own lives. One month Lisbeth took Jan, a new friend who was feeling particularly low after surgery and losing her hair due to chemotherapy. She wondered if her hair would ever grow back or if she would ever feel good again.

When Jan walked in and saw the table full of women who had survived cancer, she said: "I never would have guessed that the common bond of this table of beautiful women was breast cancer—they were happy and laughing. They were living productive lives—*and their hair had grown back!*" Being a part of that group was a significant factor in Jan's recovery.

Health Concerns for Singles

"As a single woman, I wasn't even thinking about my health until I was blind-sided by cancer," says Stacey. She quickly realized she wasn't doing the things that make for a healthy lifestyle and was also faced with the fear of how she was going to handle chemotherapy and recovery while trying to keep her job, pay bills, and take care of all her responsibilities.

"When you're single, there's no one to take care of you—to remind you to eat vegetables instead of fast food or to exercise," she says. Although her family came during her crisis to offer help and support, they had to go home, and she didn't even have the energy to pay bills or fill out insurance forms.

Here are some things she learned through the experience:

- "I had to lay down my pride and independence and learn to ask for help," says Stacey. There are resources out there—community resources, support groups, church, and Bible study—that can help you, but *asking* and *being willing to accept help* is the key. "I know I have friends who would have come over and helped me with bills and insurance if only I'd expressed the need," she adds.

- Allow God to be for you what He promises. He promises He'll be your comfort; He'll hold you up; He'll provide for your needs. "I was already His child," says Stacey. "All I had to do was to appropriate His promises." In receiving God's help and learning to lean on Him, she experienced a kind of peace she never had before.

- Your concern for parents or loved ones who might be left behind also needs to go into God's hands. For the single adult who doesn't have siblings to help with the care of aging parents, this is especially anxiety-producing. "When I was struggling with cancer, I thought, *My parents have cared for me their whole lives. Now I'm supposed to take care of them, and they are supposed to die first, not me!*" Stacy came to realize that if she was gone, God would take care of her family—He had promised!

- Without becoming overly absorbed in your health and fitness, make the effort to take better care of yourself. "I preach to myself now about living and eating healthy," says Stacey. "I do more exercising, am still working on my diet, and, without becoming a hypochondriac, am being more aware of my body (instead of ignoring symptoms or being in denial)." Many women are afraid to get a mammogram or do self-examination because they might find something suspicious. But when you catch things early, chances of successful treatment and full recovery are greater.

The Challenge of Chronic Illness

When Kathy was pregnant with her fifth child, she found herself constantly ill with flu symptoms and extreme fatigue. She couldn't make it through the grocery store without leaning against the cart four or five times. At home she lay on the couch all day except for preparing meals for her children. Each week at her appointment she asked the doctor about the fatigue and symptoms she was experiencing and asked for more tests, but she was brushed off and told she was fine.

Finally at seven months she insisted on having her blood sugars checked. The diagnosis: diabetes. Her out-of-control blood sugars posed a danger to the health of their baby. Insulin shots got her through the pregnancy, and their baby was born without birth defects or complications.

"During those last eight weeks I was told the diabetes might go away after the delivery, so I set my worry aside,"

Kathy says. She didn't want to face the possibility this could be a chronic condition. But after her baby was born, she found out she had Type II Diabetes. Now she couldn't escape reality. Diabetes was going to be with her for the rest of her life.

At first when her blood sugars were difficult to get in control, she was filled with fears about the future and possible complications the doctor had warned her about, such as damage to her eyesight or heart. The fears she was experiencing caused a high anxiety level. Because stress raises blood sugar levels, her sugars raged out of control. Coming to grips with her chronic illness and her anxiety was a must for Kathy.

Bringing It Home

How to Cope with Chronic Illness

Rely on and trust in the sovereignty of God. Kathy is choosing to rest in the knowledge of who He is and in His ultimate control over all that occurs in her life. Establishing a daily, intimate walk with Him, she chooses a moment-by-moment surrender to His perfect plan for her life.

This didn't come easy for Kathy; it was a yearlong process. Like Jacob in the Old Testament, she's a wrestler by nature. "I did a lot of wrestling with God over the *why's*. If He has the power to prevent this, why didn't He?" She also struggled with guilt, anger, and depression.

Finally Kathy relinquished control of her life and the diabetes—a realization that God is in ultimate control. Even with the diabetes that appears to be negative in her life, He has promised to use for *her good and His glory*. "I can trust Him, but it didn't come without much struggle," she says.

Along with God's sovereignty, His love for Kathy is her anchor. "I believe nothing occurs outside of His love for me, even this." She stands on Romans 8:35–39, which expresses the truth that *nothing* can remove us from the love of Christ, including illness.

Become knowledgeable about the illness. Learning about diabetes empowers Kathy to do her part while letting go of those aspects she cannot control. At times she does all that is required medically, yet still experiences high, blood sugar levels. To gain more knowledge, she looks for book and magazine resources and taps into the experiences of people facing the same illness and those with medical expertise.

Look for and enjoy the simple pleasures of daily life. "I cannot always control the quality of my life," says Kathy, "but I can determine its fullness." So she purposefully creates beauty in her surroundings, invests herself passionately in her relationships of family and friends, enjoys and celebrates daily life with her children, and takes time to nurture herself in areas of personal interests and hobbies.

Seek to maintain a balanced approach to the management of the illness without slipping into perfectionism or failing to acknowledge your humanity. Although she sticks to a rigorous diet and exercise regimen to manage her diabetes, Kathy gives herself permission to eat foods from her "no" list occasionally or to eliminate her exercise routine on any given day. Insulin shots are mandatory, but she tries to be flexible in other areas of diabetes management.

The choice of a physician has a great impact in relieving anxiety— in both the present and the future. A chronic illness demands a long-term relationship. By knowing herself and what is important to her in a doctor-patient "fit," Kathy found a doctor who showed respect and sensitivity for her desires and concerns.

Although the heavy wrestling over the whys has ended for now and Kathy has a true peace and contentment, she's aware that it's not a once-and-for-all issue. If she develops physical complications or the diabetes gets out of control, anxiety and fear may surface again. "But if I can keep coming back to my anchor of God's sovereignty and love—that's my hope," she says. She often meditates on and prays 2 Corinthians 4:16–18: "Therefore we do not lose heart, but though our outer man is decaying, yet our inner man is being renewed day by day. For momentary, light affliction is producing for us an eternal weight of glory far beyond all comparison, while we look not at the things which are seen, but at the things which are not seen; for the things which are seen are temporal, but the things which are not seen are eternal" (NASB).

Wholeness: An Ongoing Process

Dr. Kay Toombs, assistant professor of philosophy at Baylor University, lives by the Victor Frankl quote from *Man's Search for Meaning:* "Everything can be taken away from a person but the freedom to choose how to react to any given set of circumstances." She finds it incredibly freeing that no matter what happens to her body, she always has a choice about how she responds.

In 1973, when Kay was first diagnosed with multiple sclerosis (MS)—a degenerative disease of the central nervous system—she was not so confident. After suffering a temporary loss of vision in her right eye and receiving the diagnosis of MS, her first reaction was to be absolutely terrified. She left the doctor's office and called the Multiple Sclerosis Society. At the first meeting she attended, they showed a movie about a man who was diagnosed with MS and within a matter of weeks was immobilized in a wheelchair while his wife was outside hammering up a "For Sale" sign in their yard.

"I just felt like here was the blueprint for my life," Kay says. For two years after her diagnosis that movie colored her understanding of what it meant to have MS. Contemplating the grim prospects, she would go to sleep at night terrified that when she woke up, she wouldn't be able to move at all.

Turning Points: Overcoming Fear

Part of the turning point came when she realized after a couple of years that she could carry on with a relatively normal life with MS, but that she couldn't live with the paralyzing fear. The fear was even more debilitating than the illness. "Fear paralyzed me from being able to do anything," she says. So she made conscious choices to focus on the *present* instead of worrying about what was going to happen to her and how her MS was going to progress in the future. For example, rather than thinking about what degree she was going to get or if she'd be well enough to finish her M.A., she focused on getting through the particular course she was enrolled in. By focusing on the present instead of fearing the future, she obtained not only two master's degrees but a Ph.D. as well.

Illness and Anxiety

"One of the problems with serious illness is people project all kinds of fears about the future," says Kay. "What will I do if I can't get out of bed in five years, and how will I deal with it? What if my illness progresses?" These fears turn into global anxiety about everything. Since the situation is in the future and you don't know how you'd handle it, you can't deal with it, and your anxiety becomes an absolute loss of control.

Kay has found three keys to dealing with this anxiety:

First, she tries to focus on the concrete difficulties instead of the imagined ones. For example, rather than worry that she may be so weak in the future that she can't teach her university classes, she has learned to focus on the real, concrete problem: How am I going to be able to stand at the podium to lecture for forty-five minutes? Then she looks for solutions: use an overhead projector, get a lift for her chair, and so on.

The whole notion of *choice* drains away a lot of anxiety also. "What I'm going to do with my time, how I'm going to respond to MS, choices in terms of medical treatment—it's very important to know you still have choices." For example, she took chemotherapy for four months but found it made her life so dysfunctional it wasn't worth the little improvement. So she chose to stop the treatments.

Often the things we fear the most don't turn out like we'd imagined. After twenty-three years of living with MS, Kay has found that when we actually have to face what we have feared, it's not at all like we thought and usually not nearly as bad.

"One of the most terrifying things to me was the thought that I'd end up in a wheelchair. I wasted a lot of energy in fear!" she says. She is in a wheelchair now, and although she gets very irritated about how people respond to a person in a wheelchair and although there are frustrations of getting in and out of places, she still carries on her life. She teaches at the university, and she does research and all the things she wanted to do. In addition to her role as a professor, she has published thirteen chapters and articles and authored two books and spoken at the European Congress on Family Practice/Clinical Medicine in Sweden.

Humor allows you to see that difficult things have their amusing side. "I try not to take myself too seriously," Kay says. Blessed with a sense of humor, Kay looks for the light side, even in difficulties. Her lively sense of humor, as evidenced by the sticker of Kermit the Frog on her mobilized wheelchair, helps her keep a healthy perspective on things.

In Kay's work, she combines her philosophical training with firsthand experience of chronic, debilitating disease in order to teach and write on issues related to the challenges of incurable illness and the care of the chronically ill. Intersecting her career with her own life experience has contributed to her sense of purpose and fulfillment. At the heart of her life and work is a commitment to live moment to moment, making the most of each opportunity, and anticipating the best.

Lifesavers and Worrybusters

How precious it is, Lord, to realize that you are thinking about me constantly! I can't even count how many times a day your thoughts turn towards me. And when I waken in the morning, you are still thinking of me! (Ps. 139:17–18, TLB)

He knows every detail of what is happening to me.
(Job 23:10, TLB)

Be strong, and let your heart take courage,
All you who hope in the LORD. (Ps. 31:24, NASB)

Friends, when life gets really difficult, don't jump to the conclusion that God isn't on the job. Instead, be glad that you are in the very thick of what Christ experienced. This is a spiritual refining process, with glory just around the corner.
(1 Pet. 4:12–13, *The Message*)

When I am weak, then I am strong—the less I have, the more I depend on him. (2 Cor. 12:10, TLB)

The LORD is my strength and my shield;
  my heart trusts in him, and I am helped.
My heart leaps for joy
  and I will give thanks to him in song. (Ps. 28:7)

My comfort in my suffering is this:
Your promise renews my life. (Ps. 119:50)

May the God of hope fill you with all joy and peace as you trust
in him, so that you may overflow with hope by the power of
the Holy Spirit. (Rom. 15:13)

A joyful heart is good medicine,
But a broken spirit dries up the bones.
(Prov. 17:22, NASB)

It is God who arms me with strength
and makes my way perfect. (Ps. 18:32)

Surely He has borne our griefs (sicknesses, weaknesses, and
distresses) and carried our sorrows and pains. . . . But He was
wounded for our transgressions, He was bruised for our guilt
and iniquities; the chastisement needful to obtain peace and
well-being for us was upon Him, and with the stripes that
wounded Him we are healed and made whole. (Isa. 53:4–5,
AMP)

Who shall separate us from the love of Christ? Shall trouble or
hardship or persecution or famine or nakedness or danger or
sword? . . . No, in all these things we are more than conquerors
through him who loved us. For I am convinced that neither
death nor life, neither angels nor demons, neither the present
nor the future, nor any powers, neither height nor depth, nor
anything else in all creation, will be able to separate us from
the love of God that is in Christ Jesus our Lord.
(Rom. 8:35,37–39)

11

Acceptance:
The Door to Peace

*In returning to Me and resting in Me you shall be
saved; in quietness and in (trusting) confidence
shall be your strength.*
—Isaiah 30:15, AMP

Marilyn was exhausted the morning she came home from the
center where her husband, Dave, had received treatment for
alcoholism for thirty days. Every day for a month she had been
handling not only their three children, but fielding calls from
bill collectors, shuttling kids to school, working at a part-time
job, and trying to run a household. Dave emerged in better
shape than he'd been in months. Marilyn, however, was a wreck.

In her room that morning she threw a fit before God, crying and even yelling, "I've prayed since 1989 about our
finances, and You say Your Word doesn't return void." Her
tirade continued as she looked over her journal entries and
Scriptures she'd prayed and clung to in the past year, looked at
the stack of bills she couldn't pay, and sobbed in discouragement. "I just don't believe You anymore!"

Marilyn was angry at God for all the unanswered prayers.
She was angry at her friends who hadn't confronted Dave with
his alcoholism, mad at Dave for getting them in financial
trouble and for his addiction, angry at herself for putting up
with the awful situation they were in and what this had done

to their family. Most of all, she was terrified about what they were going to do now that Dave was sober but out of a job and how they would pay the huge pile of bills.

As Dave passed their bedroom and saw Marilyn on the floor, he asked, "What's the matter?"

"I don't understand these finances and why we can't ever pay our bills. I've trusted God and He's let me down," Marilyn answered, tears flowing down her cheeks.

"Remember, acceptance is the answer to all your problems," he told her, and walked on to the garage to work on the car, reiterating a principle he learned at the center.

You mean I'm supposed to accept that we don't have any money, that you're an alcoholic, that our life has crashed? she thought, and continued to cry. Then as she thought about it, she realized her focus was always so fixed on when Dave was going to change and when their financial problems would be solved that she'd never accepted anything. She had memorized and prayed pages of Scriptures, expecting that someday their finances were going to be perfect, that they were going to be able to buy a house, and God was going to fix everything. When it didn't happen, she was crushed by disappointment.

"I was trying to 'pray in' those things—I kept looking to the future when all my prayers would be answered with what I thought was the perfect solution," she adds. "It was just like what C. S. Lewis describes in the movie *Shadowlands:* 'We live in the Shadowlands. The sun is always shining somewhere else, around the bend in the road, over the brow of a hill.' I was looking over the hill!"

So Marilyn got out her journal and began to write, "Acceptance is the answer to all my problems today," and she wrote out all the problems she faced. "Lord, I've prayed, tithed, worked, and nothing has opened up to us," she continued writing.

"So I know that if You wanted to You could change things in a moment or a day. But You haven't. So I accept the way things are today, the things I can't change. I want You to show me what You're doing. I want to see You and trust You in the midst of our problems today, in the here and now."

For the first time in a long time, peace slowly began to replace the anxiety and worry she was feeling. In the process she remembered what God had done, even in the last few months. As she thought about it, the "wilderness blessings" they'd received were many. They were living in a rented house, but it was a large, lovely one, and the owners had allowed them to live there rent-free for the time being while Dave was in the treatment center and while they recovered financially.

"I'd been just like the Israelites complaining about the manna God provided in the wilderness," she says. When you are always looking down the road from the Shadowlands, you miss what God is doing today.

She also began to see God was doing something in her and her husband, teaching them a deeper level of responsibility; changes had happened in Dave. She remembered the friends who'd supported and helped them: the ones who brought meals, the friend who gave her beautiful clothes when she had no money to buy any.

Her anxiety and anger dissipated as acceptance and gratefulness grew.

As Hannah Hurnard says, the only way to live victoriously in the midst of life's difficulties is "by learning to accept, day by day, the actual conditions and tests permitted by God, by a continually repeated laying down of our own will and acceptance of His as it is presented to us in the form of the people with whom we have to live and work, and in the things which happen to us. Every acceptance of His will becomes an altar of sacrifice, and every such surrender and abandonment of ourselves to His will is a means of furthering us on the way to the High Places to which He desires to bring every child of His while they are still living on earth."[1]

--=◎=--

Faith is . . .
Letting go of my demands that
another change and looking to God
for the change He sees I need.
—Pamela Reeve

--=◎=--

When Emotions Overwhelm

From that point several years ago to the present, whenever Marilyn begins getting anxious or emotional about any situation in her, her children's, or her family's life, she repeats the process that brings her to acceptance. No, the circumstances haven't changed overnight. But she's learned to walk in a daily peace and vibrant joy right in the midst of the problems she faces.

Here are a few simple steps that you can use when emotions rage:

- Get your journal out and start a page with "Acceptance is the answer to all my problems today."

- Then list your needs, problems, and what is causing you the most frustration.

- Think of what God is asking you to do. Perhaps you are to stop charging on your credit cards, get help from a financial counselor, and live on a budget.

- Also include the things you can't change today. If there is a nagging irritation with a person or situation, that's a good indication you are not accepting it. For example, if you are constantly irritated that your husband is not a sharp dresser, then you're not accepting him. If the house you live in is a continual burr under your saddle, then you're probably not accepting your house as God's present provision.

- As you list these, think through them: Can I change that in any way? Have I prayed about it? Could God change it if He wanted to? Have I asked Him to change it or show me my part to do? Is He asking me to do something? Is He listening? Am I listening?

- Then write what God's Word says about those things. Jot down the verses that come to mind. For example: "God has surely listened and heard my voice in prayer. Praise be to God, who has not rejected my prayer or withheld his love from me!" (Ps. 66:19–20).

⋆══◉══⋆

*True praise is not an attempt to manipulate God
into producing the precise results we hope for.
Instead it helps us accept our situation as it is,
whether or not He changes it. And if we continue
praising God, it helps us reach the place where we
can say, "Father, I don't want You to remove this
problem until You've done all You want to
do through it, in me and others."*
—Ruth Myers

⋆══◉══⋆

- Accepting is realizing you can trust God—to bring an answer, though perhaps not the answer you'd expected, *and* bring something good out of the situation or problem. Acceptance doesn't mean you quit praying, become irresponsible, or give up. It is knowing that if you are tuned in to God and His Word, *and asking Him*, He will show you your part. But if there is nothing you can do to change today's situation, acceptance is trusting God to get you through anything. As James 1:4 says, "Don't try to get out of anything prematurely. Let it do its work so you become mature and well-developed, not deficient in any way" (*The Message*).

- Acceptance is facing the difficulties and storms of life with God's peace. It will bring you into the reality of the *now* (instead of the far-off or fantasy) and allow you to see more of what God is doing and what He's called you to today. At the same time, walking in acceptance and trusting in God will drain away your fear and anxiety.

- Practice the Serenity Prayer: God, grant me the serenity to accept the things I cannot change, the courage to change the things I can, and the wisdom to know the difference.

The Spirit of Acceptance: Embracing God's Will

Fenelon, in his wonderful volume of letters entitled *Let Go*, written in the seventeenth century, captures the spirit of acceptance, or what he calls a spirit of nonresistance: "If you recognize the hand of God, and make no opposition to His will, you will have peace in the midst of affliction. Happy indeed are they who can bear their sufferings with this simple peace and perfect submission to the will of God."[2]

What Acceptance Is Not: Being a Doormat

Sometimes we equate "acceptance" with an attitude of "anything goes": "I'll accept any behavior my husband or children dish out." Instead, acceptance is embracing and dealing with the problem behavior while loving the person. For example, if you discover your son has a drug problem, acceptance is admitting he has a drug problem. Not accepting it is denial. If you're accepting the problem, you are

- there to get him help, which may involve loving confrontation and arranging for treatment,
- accepting him as a person, but not his behavior,
- setting boundaries at home,
- listening to the needs of the heart.

All the while, you are loving him unconditionally in that sickness; doing whatever common sense, God's wisdom, and reliable counsel advises you to do. None of the above includes being a doormat for your son, enabling his behavior to continue.

Make a Commitment to Wholly Trust God

How can you and I have quietness and confidence in the midst of a crisis? How can we face whatever difficulty comes with *acceptance* rather than *resignation*?

A look at the story in Daniel 3 gives us an answer. Three Israelite men—Shadrach, Meschach, and Abednego—were being thrown into the fiery furnace because they refused to bow to the Babylonian idols. They faced a terrible crisis as severe as any we might ever encounter in life. And if God didn't come and deliver them, they would die. Here's how they were able to walk through the trial without fear: In addition to all their prayer and worship of God, they had made a commitment.

> "[They] replied to the king, 'O Nebuchadnezzar, we do not need to defend ourselves before you in this matter. If we are thrown into the blazing furnace, the God we serve is able to save us from it, and he will rescue us from your hand. . . . But even if He does not, we want you to know, O king, that we will not serve your gods, or worship the image of gold you have set up.'" (Dan. 3:16–18)

David Wilkerson concludes that we are always to pray in faith, believing that God will answer; yet we are to trust Him completely with our situation, saying in our hearts, "But if not, Lord, I'm still going to trust You!"[3] That's acceptance at its deepest level: knowing Christ will come into our crisis and walk through it with us. Whatever happens, He's faithful, and *He'll never leave us or forsake us*. The peace and freedom from fear that comes with this kind of confidence in God is sufficient for any of our trials.

Bringing It Home

Ways to Accept Your Situation

Write in your journal the things and people in your life (including their behaviors) you have the hardest time accepting. Take a good, honest look at not only what you have difficulty accepting in your life, but also what fears are connected to each. With each of those issues, write the Acceptance activity described earlier in this chapter.

Shift from questioning God, "When are You going to take this problem away?" to asking Him, "What is it You're shaping in my life through this trial or difficulty?" What can I learn from this experience? Ask God to show you what He's trying to shape in your life. This kind of teachable attitude diffuses the little nagging fears and anxieties and minimizes the frustrations we feel when the wilderness season we're in continues long past when we feel it should be over.

Cultivate a sense of humor, a lightheartedness about yourself and your problems. Try even to laugh at yourself once in a while. When we look at ourselves and our problems too seriously, we become difficult to live with. A lively sense of humor helps us accept ourselves and become more accepting of others. It is *good news* that God loves and accepts us in spite of our problems and failures. Pray for that kind of "love that covers" for the people in your life.

Develop a sense of gratitude and wonder about life. Each day is a gift of God that we haven't earned or deserved, so there is always something to celebrate: a glowing purple and red sunset; the note your child left on your pillow that said, "I love you, Mom!". . . a juicy piece of watermelon to eat on a hot day . . . the first snowfall. . . . Just like the expectant wonder you felt about Christmas, delight in God's blessings every day. No matter what the difficulties are each day, there is something to celebrate. Find new things to delight in and to amaze you— little things as well as the big blessings.

→═◎═←

Acceptance says, "True, this is my situation at the moment.
I'll look unblinkingly at the reality of it. But I'll also open
my hands to accept whatever a loving Father sends."
—Catherine Marshall

→═◎═←

Lifesavers and Worrybusters

Be satisfied with your present [circumstances and with what you have]; for He (God) Himself has said, [I will] not in any way fail you nor give you up, nor leave you without support. [I will] not, [I will] not, [I will not] in any degree leave you helpless, nor forsake nor let [you] down, [relax My hold on you].— Assuredly not! So we take comfort and are encouraged and confidently and boldly say, The Lord is my Helper, I will not be seized with alarm—I will not fear or dread or be terrified. What can man do to me? (Heb. 13:5–6, AMP)

Let everyone bless God and sing his praises, for he holds our lives in his hands. And he holds our feet to the path.
(Ps. 66:8, TLB)

Do you want more and more of God's kindness and peace? Then learn to know him better and better. For as you know him better, he will give you, through his great power, everything you need for living a truly good life: he even shares his own glory and his own goodness with us! And by that same mighty power he has given us all the other rich and wonderful blessings he promised. (2 Pet. 1:2–4, TLB)

When a man is gloomy, everything seems to go wrong; when he is cheerful, everything seems right! (Prov. 15:15, TLB)

Mary . . . sat at the Lord's feet listening to what he said. But Martha was distracted by all the preparations that had to be made. . . . "Martha, Martha," the Lord answered, "you are worried and upset about many things, but only one thing is needed. Mary has chosen what is better, and it will not be taken away from her." (Luke 10:39–41)

After you have suffered a little while, our God, who is full of kindness through Christ, will give you his eternal glory. He personally will come and pick you up, and set you firmly in place, and make you stronger than ever. (1 Pet. 5:10, TLB)

He has showered down upon us the richness of his grace—for how well he understands us and knows what is best for us at all times. (Eph. 1:8, TLB)

12

Adventures in Praise:
How a Lifestyle of Praise
Turns Worry to Wonder

*Angels listen for your songs, for your voice rises to
the very gates of heaven when you praise Me.*
—Frances J. Roberts

It was the dead of winter, and we were living in Yarmouth, Maine. Discouragement was trying to wrap itself around my neck like ivy twining around a house—ivy growing so thick that if left untamed could cover the brick and windows and shut out the light. My husband was out of work and depressed. Day after day he interviewed for jobs and didn't get them. Rejections added to his discouragement. He wanted to return to Oklahoma City, but there seemed to be no way financially. He seemed to have lost hope in life.

Normally optimistic and able to encourage him, I was struggling. Every day that went by my face grew longer. I felt tired, anxious, burdened by stress. I didn't see how we could pay our bills. The long-term effects of stress, anxiety, and worry were taking their toll. Joy seemed gone from our lives, and hope seemed far away. I continued reading my Bible and talking to God in this wilderness season, but my eyes kept landing on the circumstances. I poured out my heart to Him but heard no answers.

Finally one night I shared with our Monday night Bible study group how trying a time it was for us. They prayed for us that night, but things only got worse financially, and my anxiety grew. A few weeks later at the Monday group, one of the women, Linda, took me aside and said: "Cheri, no matter how hard things are, you must praise and thank God in the midst of your circumstances. And that's not a message from me but from my missionary friend Anne. She wants you to know she's praying for you."

I had heard Linda talk about this elderly missionary who'd served in China before World War II and survived prison camp, but I didn't even know her. However, I knew Linda was right and that was what the Bible said, but it was a hard message to hear that particular night, one that pierced my heart. *I always thought You wanted genuine, not fake, praise, Lord, and I want to be real with You. How can I thank and praise You when I feel so sad inside, so discouraged? I know it's the right thing to do, so what's wrong with me?*

Visit to a Missionary

I pondered that question all week, trying to force myself to praise and thank God, but I was failing. I wanted with all my heart to be faithful but felt overwhelmed by my feelings and drained from trying to bolster my depressed husband. Falling deeper into discouragement, the next week I told Linda, "When you go to see your missionary friend this week, I want to go with you. I have a few questions I want to ask her." I thought if anyone could shed some light on my problem, this wise missionary could.

Driving along on that bitter cold December day, discouragement still covered me like a heavy blanket.

"There's their apartment up at the top of the hill next to the Catholic church," Linda said, driving into a parking space.

We walked in and were greeted warmly by Netta Anton, a Scottish nurse in her seventies who cared for the missionary lady. *That must be Anne in the brown chair*, I thought. A white-haired woman in a burgundy sweater lay in a recliner. Her legs were propped up and covered with a small green blanket. Print house shoes peeked out from the blanket.

Above Anne hung an embroidered plaque with the words, "Let us exalt the Lord together." Another said "Jesus First." A humidifier hummed. After taking our coats, Netta and Linda went in the other room to wrap Christmas packages for mailing to the missionaries they supported. This little apartment, Linda had told me, was like a shipping and receiving department. Now I was seeing it for myself. Although Netta and Anne had very little financially, they held nothing back from God. They regularly gave to many missionaries and ministries and were remembering each with a Scripture calendar this holiday.

Questions

Anne was almost totally blind, but her spiritual eyes were sharp as she looked over in my direction. She spoke with effort but a quiet authority, asking me all about our situation. She seemed to have a knowledge and understanding about my life far beyond what I shared, and after listening, she offered insights, "For your children's and husband's sakes, you must praise and thank God and *show* in your countenance your faith in Him. For he who trusts Him wholly finds Him wholly true.

"Thank Him in all things," she continued. "Praise Him even if tears are running down your cheeks."

I nodded but grimaced inside, thinking this sounded like the hardest thing to do. "But how?" I asked. "I want to praise and thank God, and I've tried, but it's so hard when I'm depressed."

"By trusting Him implicitly," she added. "You can't depend on your feelings; they are Satan's playground. *Ask for God's grace to praise Him, and He'll give it to you.*"

A few moments later Linda and Netta came in with our coats and began to bundle Anne up to prepare to leave for the restaurant. As painstakingly slow and difficult as it was with Anne's diabetic condition and leg complications, she needed to get out once a day and walk with her walker, so back out into the cold we went. One of us walked on each side of the elderly woman, our arm under hers.

❈

Praise is the soil
in which joy thrives.
—Anonymous

❈

Anne's Life in China

Over our salads and bowls of soup, I asked about Anne's experiences as a missionary in China. She shared about the day she was to leave Shanghai for furlough in Scotland. After nine years of service with the China Inland Mission, Anne couldn't wait to see her mother, family, and friends back in Scotland. She was overdue for a respite. She and the other missionaries had packed all their belongings and were about to leave for the boat when Anne heard a clamor outside their dormitory.

As she watched out the mission house window, she saw Japanese soldiers goose-stepping in unison down the street, knees almost up to their noses. The Lord spoke to her heart, "Come aside for a moment. I want to talk to you, Anne." Reminding her of His care and provision in many adventures and close calls in the nine years she ministered in China, He told her she was not going home but would be a prisoner of the Japanese. He didn't tell her how long but said He would be with her.

A precious but very real sense of God's nearness and peace filled her as the Lord spoke. "I've never forgotten this overwhelming peace and the Lord's closeness to me in that moment," Anne said. Then He asked her, "Do you have any prayer requests to make?"

Although Anne had never given her teeth a thought, the Holy Spirit nudged her to pray that her teeth would be preserved and not one of them fall out. (Often the health and diet of prisoners is so bad that they lose their teeth.) So out of obedience rather than vanity, she asked God to protect her teeth.

Moments later she and the other English and American missionaries were taken prisoner and marched off to a Japanese prison camp. There she spent three and a half years in near-starvation, dreadful cold in winter, and scorching heat in summer. Cruelty, rats, disease, and death were all around her. There were no Bibles, so she had to rely on all the verses she had committed to memory.

Rat Patrol

"The very first night I had a visitor," Anne said with a sparkle in her eye. Waking up with a startle in the middle of the night, she saw a big rat asleep up her sleeve. Scared to death, she almost screamed but remembered the Japanese guards outside the door and the severe punishment they had promised for any disturbance. When she turned to God, her only resource, He seemed to say, "Imagine how you look when you sleep!" That thought made her smile. Just then the rat woke up and scampered out her sleeve to join the other rats congregating under the bottom of the bed below her.

"The next day I organized a 'rat patrol' to club as many rats as we could and make the barracks a safer place for the other women and children," Anne said with a chuckle. She shared about God's constant presence, of the people who came to know Christ. She counted it all joy. She seemed to possess this quiet assurance she could absolutely trust God because He was worthy. She could count on Him, and she knew He would never fail her.

Story after story she related about God's provision for her in the prison camp. I sat there spellbound, marveling at the mercy and faithfulness of the God she and I serve.

Anne was released after World War II ended. And although she was in poor health at the close of internment, every single tooth was preserved. But other losses awaited her. Anne was told her mother died while she was in prison camp. Although she never got to see her again, there was no bitterness about the past. And though she was dealing with the day-to-day trials of aging, her eyes failing and suffering several surgeries, she encouraged us: "Trust. Cast all your cares on Him. No matter what's on your mind, roll it onto His shoulders and rest under His wing."

Before we left the restaurant, Anne searched in her purse and brought out a small tract that she placed with the tip for our waitress. "Never leave home without your ammunition," Anne told Linda and me. "You never know how many people will be in heaven because of reading the gospel in a tract you handed them." She was prayerful over which tract to give, just like they prayed over everything, continually communicating with God and listening to His voice. She lived to make Christ known to others—in every appointment, every person that crossed her path or came to the apartment. *That's where those piercing questions she asked and the telescopic view she seemed to have into my life must have come from—being in constant communion with Him*, I thought.

Tea Time

Our visit continued after the return to their toasty apartment. Netta brought out an old English tray with a steaming pot of tea and crisp gingersnaps for their daily "Tea Time" before our trip back to Yarmouth.

On the drive home, my thoughts were filled with Anne's stories and the Scriptures she had shared. Her words came back to me: "Don't lean on your own understanding. Don't trust what you see or feel or think; trust God and His Word. He's faithful even when we're not." I prayed silently, "Lord, I want to praise and thank You right in the middle of our situation, and I ask for Your grace to do that."

The Turnaround

That night my husband was just as withdrawn and depressed as usual, but something new was engaging my thoughts. The next few days in my quiet time I searched the Scriptures, especially the Psalms, for words to praise God. All the feelings of discouragement and worry were still lurking around, trying to drag me down, but I knelt and used these verses to "adore Him." This time I didn't wait until I felt better.

As I did, that deep heaviness began to lift, the anxiety about our empty checking account lifted with it. It was as if dark glasses were removed and I saw what I'd never seen before: that no matter how difficult or trying our situation was and even if *nothing* external changed, I could praise and thank God because the trial would only draw me into a closer relationship with Him.

Like a trickle from a frozen creek in the spring, something deep inside me began to thaw, and thanksgiving bubbled up and flowed. Slowly at first, my perspective began to change. I enjoyed loving God for the first time in a long time—no list of requests, no complaints. I could thank God for the season and for the inner work He was doing in us. I thanked Him for our health, for our children, our marriage that was still together (and even the fact that it had been strained had drawn me closer to depend on God), for the plan He had for my husband, though we hadn't seen it—even for the financial losses because they reminded me of the temporariness of material things and our eternal treasures in Christ.

❖⟳❖

> *Praise is the Christian's artillery.*
> *Praise is more effective in spiritual warfare*
> *than an atomic bomb in military battle—*
> *far more effective.*
> —*Fern Nichols*

❖⟳❖

A Lifestyle of Praise

"God uses tough situations to draw you nearer to Him and to enrich your praise," says Ruth Myers, a missionary with The Navigators in Singapore since 1970.[1] A lifestyle of praise doesn't mean you deny your real feelings, she adds. You may be experiencing intense feelings of fear or sorrow. It's expressing your distressing emotions to God yet choosing to keep praising in spite of how things look to you—and not postponing praise until you feel better. It's developing a faith that goes beyond your feelings.

At first you may start to praise God with little trickles as I did, but if you persist, even in the darkest of places, you will find those trickles of faith will turn into a fountain of praise. Keep praising, and watch your attitude turn from anxiety and worry to wonder. You'll even begin to see your situation differently: "Praise can heighten your awareness that distressing circumstances are God's blessings in disguise. Your trials rip away the flimsy fabric of your self-sufficiency. This makes room for God's Spirit to weave into your life a true and solid confidence—the kind of confidence that Paul expressed in Philippians 4:13: 'I can do all things through Christ who strengthens me'" (Phil. 4:13, NKJV).[2]

I love what Fern Nichols, founder and president of Moms in Touch International, says about praise: Praise lifts our eyes from the battle to the victor. Praise drives away frustration, tension, depression, and fear. Are you shaken? Start praising. Praise cleanses the atmosphere, gets rid of all the smog and fog so that we can see clearly who is in control. Our focus is drawn from the complexity of the problem to the adequacy of God's infinite resources.[3]

"Bloom where you're planted" is a happy thought, but have you ever been "pruned back" from being in such a season of extended trials that you didn't know if you'd ever bloom again?

One April morning when we were living in Maine, I walked our Sheltie down the road. It had snowed for days, and everything was frozen. The barren trees stood stark against the white fields we passed. In the entire month there had been only twenty-four hours of sun! A somber gray sky above offered little promise of a break in the wintry weather.

Yet for this Texas girl, winter had lasted too long. I was deep into light deprivation. I thought of the gorgeous pink and red azalea bushes blooming in Dallas that my sister described to me on the phone the night before. I was longing for spring—and also for things to turn around in our lives.

Just then I noticed a rose bush that had been severely cut back before the snow covered it. Now it was stark, with ice solidly frozen around it. Our lives, too, had been pruned, and the struggles weren't going away. Three months had gone by after my visit to Anne, the missionary, and I wondered when the turnaround was coming; we were feeling isolated living two thousand miles away from friends and family. Holmes was still having a tough time in business and no new construction to work on. We had lost our house back home, and our savings were gone. We hadn't found a church to be involved in, so we felt useless. I thought, *That's what we're like; we've been pruned too, a not altogether painless process.*

But just like this rose bush, you will bloom again and be fruitful, God seemed to say. *Let your roots go down deep in Me. Praise Me in the winters too!*

As I did, I slowly began to realize that praising and thanking God—no matter how difficult things get—will help us bloom again. There's no hole we can get ourselves into that's too deep for His love to fill. And the tough times, whether financial or physical, press us into a deeper, more intimate relationship with Him. Just as the roots of a plant grow deeper in the winter to anchor it, our faith and dependence on God are strengthened in our "winters."

It's easy to praise God in the summer when there's fruit on the vine and life looks great, but it takes faith to praise God in the winter when—as it says in Habakkuk 3:17—there are no buds on the trees, the crops have failed, the flocks are lost, and the fields produce no food. Take heart, you will bloom again, with greater fruit than before! Just keep anchoring yourself in Christ and trust Him to bring a springtime or resurrection in your life.

Bringing It Home

- Read the story for yourself in 2 Chronicles 20:1–30 and write in your journal the insights you find on praise, worship, and God's intervention that you can directly apply to your situation.

• Get *31 Days of Praise* by Ruth Myers (published by The Navigators, Orchard P. O. Box 824, Singapore 9123). There is a praise page or paragraph for each day of the month to develop your praise life. Read one praise paragraph each day, silently or even aloud at the dinner table. These personalized Scripture praise sections will refresh your quiet time and build your confidence in God.

• If you find that feelings of despair, guilt, fear, or anger are hindering your praise, open that very problem or issue up to God. Pour out your heart to Him about what is bothering you—moving toward God instead of away from Him.

Lifesavers and Worrybusters

Both of the following translations of Colossians 2:6–7 are wonderful:

As you therefore have received Christ Jesus the Lord, so walk in Him, having been firmly rooted and now being built up in Him and established in your faith, just as you were instructed, and overflowing with gratitude. (NASB)

Now just as you trusted Christ to save you, trust him, too, for each day's problems; live in vital union with him. Let your roots grow down into him and draw up nourishment from him. See that you go on growing in the Lord, and become strong and vigorous in the truth you were taught. Let your lives overflow with joy and thanksgiving for all he has done. (TLB)

"I am the vine, you are the branches; he who abides in Me, and I in him, he bears much fruit; for apart from Me you can do nothing. . . . If you abide in Me, and My words abide in you, ask whatever you wish, and it shall be done for you. By this is My Father glorified, that you bear much fruit, and so prove to be My disciples." (John 15:5,7–8, NASB)

With Jesus' help we will continually offer our sacrifice of praise to God by telling others of the glory of his name. (Heb. 13:15, TLB)

True praise is a worthy sacrifice; this really honors me. Those who walk my paths will receive salvation from the Lord. (Ps. 50:23, TLB)

O magnify the LORD with me,
And let us exalt His name together.
I sought the LORD, and He answered me,
And delivered me from all my fears.
They looked to Him and were radiant,
And their faces shall never be ashamed.
(Ps. 34:3–5, NASB)

Though the fig tree does not bud
    and there are no grapes on the vines,
though the olive crop fails
    and the fields produce no food,
though there are no sheep in the pen,
    and no cattle in the stalls,
yet I will rejoice in the LORD,
    I will be joyful in God my Savior.
(Hab. 3:17)

Why are you in despair, O my soul?
And why have you become disturbed within me?
Hope in God, for I shall again praise Him
For the help of His presence.
(Ps. 42:5, NASB)

Hallelujah! Yes, praise the Lord!

Praise him in his Temple, and in the heavens he made with mighty power. Praise him for his mighty works. Praise his unequaled greatness. . . .

Let everything alive give praises to the Lord! You praise him! (Ps. 150:1–6, TLB)

13

Ten Ways to Live the Adventure: How to Embrace Change and Follow God's Guidance

The early disciples were called to leave their families and the comfort and security of familiar ways and places. . . . Day by day they discovered that life was a great adventure, and that every hardship and every setback was a doorway to new service and maturity.
—KEITH MILLER AND BRUCE LARSEN

One Sunday night in 1978 Holmes and I were gathering up our Bibles and *The Edge of Adventure* books after a small group we were leading in our church had dispersed when a woman in the group approached us.

"You really seem to believe all that," she observed.

"All what?" I asked. "The material we discussed tonight in our small group?"

"No, I mean you really believe the Bible is true, don't you? You seem to be applying this stuff—like it's not just a myth or story, but something you can build your whole life on," she added.

"Yes, we do. That's what makes life so exciting," I answered.

For us, the Adventure had begun. And as I've shared in the previous chapters, we began to be transformed as a result of our renewed relationship with Christ and our pursuit of God. As a result, our marriage changed (slowly but surely). Our priorities changed. And as a result of our following God, both our careers changed, and we've both been self-employed since that year.

The biggest change of all was that we found life to be a day-by-day adventure and that God had a different purpose for us from what we'd planned.

Ten Principles to Living the Adventure

1. *Show up for service!* When you present yourself as a living sacrifice as Romans 12:1 directs, be ready for the Adventure to accelerate, for God is looking for *willing vessels.* "For the eyes of the LORD range throughout the earth to strengthen those whose hearts are fully committed to him" (2 Chron. 16:9).

We are the vessels—not perfect ones, but willing ones. "But we have this treasure in jars of clay to show that this all-surpassing power is from God and not from us" (2 Cor. 4:7).

Showing up for service also means connecting with God each morning: "Here's my life, my hands, my emotions and will, my intellect—all that I am. Use me today in whatever way You want. Give me a specific word of encouragement for someone who needs it. Show me how I can serve, help, comfort someone. No matter how small the task, here I am—use me!"

God has a special purpose and mission for your life, and He has gifted you to fulfill that purpose. Review chapter 8 on "Soaring with Your Talents" and do some of the exercises at the end to help identify your gifts and purpose. As you give yourself to God with an abondon and surrender, you'll begin to find the purpose or mission you were created for doing in this particular season of your life. You may need more training or preparation. But whether it is painting pictures, programming computers, administrating a business or ministry, teaching and nurturing children, inventing something, dancing, singing, or composing music—He has gifted you and equipped you to fulfill the very purpose He made you for.

2. *Take one step at a time.* When you know what your interest or gifts are, what you enjoy doing, or what God is calling you to (i.e., what you're passionate about), it's time to begin following the guidance He gives you.

Psalm 119:105 says His Word will light our path. It's a promise! When God shows you a step to take and you take it, He will give you the light you need for the next step. I find He rarely reveals the whole blueprint—more often He reveals the next step in His plan.

Paul writes, "We are His workmanship, created in Christ Jesus for good works, which God prepared beforehand, that we should walk in them" (Eph. 2:10, NASB). He has planned things for you and me to do—ahead of time, before we ever thought about them! I believe there are songs in heaven God is looking for someone to write, stories He wants told, missionary projects He has in mind. He's already thought of them in heaven and wants willing vessels to accomplish them on earth.

⊷═◉═⊷

Do not despise this small beginning.
—*Zechariah 4:10,* TLB

⊷═◉═⊷

But just like a miner's hat, which casts a beam six feet ahead to give enough light to illuminate his next steps, until we walk those six feet, we won't be able to see more of the path. This is one of the strategies for finding God's direction we discovered in *The Edge of Adventure.*[1] Taking the steps often involves risk. In fact, someone said that "Faith" is spelled "R-I-S-K."

One day Louise Montgomery was waiting for her car to be repaired in a small town in Maine when into the auto shop strolled Alison Kelley. The two women, who had never met, began chatting. Soon they discovered that although they were twenty years apart in age, they had much in common, especially the fact that both were strong believers in the power of prayer. The two became prayer partners.

Alison, a registered nurse, often spoke to Louise about her volunteer work at a shelter for the homeless in Boston. "As we talked and prayed," Louise said, "I became convinced God wanted me to try to open a shelter in Portland."

And so by following the guidance God was giving her, Louise and her husband, both in their mid-seventies, took their life savings of $50,000 and began combing Portland for a big house. "You'll never find a house for that money," real estate agents told them.

But God had given Louise a dream, a picture of what He wanted her to do, and find one they did—a fourteen-room dilapidated structure. Restoring it was a huge project, but as they prayed, Louise felt directed to ask for help from the Cumberland County Jail. After many objections, the city finally agreed to lend the jail's manpower. With the inmates' help, the Montgomerys restored the ceilings and floors, replaced broken windows, replastered, and painted the three-story house. Many obstacles presented themselves, but after prayer and more light on the path, they always found a way. And God provided. Claude, a noted artist, traded one of his paintings for appliances. Their daughter gave a new furnace. More funds were needed in order to open the shelter. For weeks, Louise went to churches of all faiths and returned with contributions of blankets, furniture, food, and money.

The night before Christmas Eve 1985, Friendship House opened its doors to serve the homeless with a graciousness and love their "guests" never dreamed of. Ever since then it has been a home for thousands of homeless people without charge—a place of healing, recovery, and hope.

Several years later, the Montgomerys, now almost eighty years old, saw a need for a shelter especially for women. After months of prayer and following God's guidance, Faith House was established nearby in downtown Portland. And even after Louise and Claude died, their daughter, Susan, and her husband continue the work of Friendship House and Faith House.

Although your "steps" may be different from Louise's, the same principles apply—because God has a plan for you that He promises to reveal if you're looking, listening, and following His guidance. "I will instruct you and teach you in the way you should go. I will counsel you and watch over you" (Ps. 32:8).

God will provide the guidance and show you the steps to take, but He wants you to do your part *to follow His light*.

⊷═◉═⊷

We are not at our best perched at the summit;
we are climbers, at our best when the way is deep.
—*John W. Gardner*

⊷═◉═⊷

Once your boat is in the water, don't get caught on the sandbar of discouragement. *Keep moving!* The old saying is true: You can't pilot a moored ship, especially one stuck in the dock. If God gives you an idea or a dream, get your sailboat in the water so the Holy Spirit can move your rudder and blow His wind on your sails. As one writer friend says, "I have yet to have an editor appear on my doorstep with a check and ask me for an article." We've got to plant seeds, move, prepare, work—doing our part and trusting God to do His. And one of the ways He does His part to direct us is to open and close doors.

Ask God to open and close doors and *be ready for both!* That's how He moves your rudder; but when the closed doors, or no's, come, keep going. Bounce back from discouragement—don't let it paralyze you.

"I'm a door-rattler," says my friend Norma Jean. She says, "If you want to close the door, Lord, that's fine. But I'm going to shake them all!" When she tries an idea that doesn't work, she doesn't stay flattened. "I've gotten knocked down a lot. Each time I get up a little quicker and run a little faster."

If you are looking for direction, read the Bible daily and let God speak to you through it. It's a major source of guidance. Read it to discover His will. The Bible is speaking today. And if you want to know God better, hear His direction, and learn His ways of living, open your Bible daily with great expectations. Before you read, ask: What is this passage saying about God? about me? What do I hear God nudging me to do today? The Bible "is more than a thing, it is a voice, a word, the very Word of the living God," says A. W. Tozer.[2]

3. *Say yes in advance.* If there's a decision to be made or a fork in the road and you are asking God to show you the way to go, sign on the dotted line of your contract with God *in advance*, even before you know what He's going to have you do. Say as Jehoshaphat did, "[I] do not know what to do, but [my] eyes are upon you"—If you show me, I'll commit in advance to whatever You direct! (2 Chron. 20:12, NIV).

Does this sound scary or difficult? Are you afraid if you say yes that God will send you to some remote place you always dreaded or have you do a job you hate? This may come from the notion that God is a mean Killjoy just waiting to spoil our fun. It's just the opposite of the truth: "No eye has seen, no ear has heard, no mind has conceived what God has prepared for those who love him" (1 Cor. 2:9).

You see, God's will is not a terrible or burdensome thing— it's the greatest thing to discover in all of life. It's the Greatest Adventure of a lifetime to walk with Him and do what He's planned.

Signing in advance is a way of giving up any areas you're holding out, saying, "I'll go anywhere, but not *there*." It's admitting that you are joyfully committing yourself to God and to what He chooses for your life.

Even in uncertain situations I feel encouraged that God is the best person to write in the blank spaces because He's the only One who knows the future. We can't see around the corner as He can. He has the whole blueprint, and *this* Father really knows best! I find when I sign in advance, it facilitates discovering what His will is. I actually do this on a page in my journal, drawing lines, writing my commitment to follow God if He will "fill in the blanks," to reveal His plan or the next step; and then I sign my name.

4. *We're not on this trail alone.* God doesn't mean for us to be Lone Rangers. He shows His faithfulness in sending people to encourage, speak truth, and be "Jesus with skin on." We're part of the body of Christ, and we need the other members.

That's one of the reasons we're all a combination of both strengths and weaknesses and why nobody is strong in every single area. God planned it this way so that we need each other: "Just as there are many parts to our bodies, so it is with Christ's body. We are all parts of it, and it takes every one of us to make it complete, for we each have different work to do. So we belong to each other, and each needs all the others. God has given each of us the ability to do certain things well" (Rom. 12:4–6, TLB).

Prayer support and the counsel of trusted Christians on the Adventure trail is crucial. In addition, the other members of the body need our encouragement: our hugs, smiles, thoughtful notes, and cards that show our appreciation for their gifts or what God did through them. We all go through times when we have been battered about in a storm, have lost someone or something dear to us, or felt alone. So we all need encouragement.

In addition, look at those who have gone before us in this Adventure of Faith. Of course, there are those in the Hall of Fame in Hebrews 12: Noah, who believed God and built the ark He commanded him to; Abraham, who left his home and went far away to the land God promised to give him; Jacob and Joseph, Moses and Joshua, and other people of great faith.

But also look at the lives of biblical women who could have feared but trusted God: Sarah, who because of her faith followed her husband but was able to become a mother in old age. Esther, whom God had brought into the palace "for just such a time as this" to save the nation of Israel, responded with faith and dependence on God. Ruth, who though widowed at a young age sought refuge under the wings of God. She left her own country and people to live with Naomi, her mother-in-law, in a foreign country. Deborah, Rahab, Mary, Elizabeth—all are part of that great cloud of witnesses cheering us on in this Adventure of Faith. Read their stories and remember: you are not alone!

5. *We are going to make mistakes on the Adventure, even when we're trying to follow God's will.* But God turns ashes into beauty

(see Isa. 61:3). He has a wonderful way of turning our mourning into joy and making bitter experiences sweet. He redeems our mistakes and the mistakes of others to weave them into a pattern of good for our lives. Even what the enemy means for evil and destruction, God uses for good—just look at the life of Joseph.

Perhaps you only see jagged lines across your life or a fragmented mess. Just as an artist can redeem a seemingly ruined painting with his brush strokes, how much more can God's love and power make beauty out of blunders, bring strength out of our weaknesses, change failures into successes.

We can move from "Victim" or "Failure" when we give God our mistakes (confessing our own errors and asking for His help) and the mistakes of others who have hurt us. "We are hard-pressed on all sides, but we are never frustrated; we are puzzled, but never in despair. We are persecuted, but are never deserted: we may be knocked down but we are never knocked out! Every day we experience something of the death of Jesus, so that we may also show the power of the life of Jesus in these bodies of ours" (2 Cor. 4:7–8, Phillips).

6. *Don't let bitterness or envy, unforgiveness or self-pity eat away at your roots and weaken them.* When my friend Flo Perkins went through a particularly difficult time of her life, her daughter and two grandchildren were living with them. Her husband was deeply depressed and unable to work, and she was working long hours including weekends and holidays to support them all. Her strength was almost spent, and she wondered where God was.

Late one night a fierce winter rainstorm raged outside. As the wind howled and lightning flashed, she looked out in the dark to check on her young peach tree. Flo was troubled to see her little tree wrestling with the wind and rain. Back and forth, back and forth, it went, bending nearly to the ground.

My little tree will surely be subdued and broken by morning, she thought, finally falling into a restless sleep. But the next morning, to her surprise the storm had spent itself, but her peach tree stood tall and calm, basking in the morning sunlight. It seemed untroubled by the fierce battle it had experienced the night before. And somehow seeing that the peach tree had survived the storm, she knew that God would be sufficient and provide the strength she needed to stand.

She was also reminded that trees are created to bend with the storm and bounce back unless they are diseased or improperly planted. Our "roots" must be deep in God's Word if we are going to withstand the wind and storms, free from the disease of resentment or whatever would hinder us from following God and bending with the storms of life.

Hebrews 12:15 says, "See to it that no one misses the grace of God and that no bitter root grows up to cause trouble and defile many" (NASB). Keeping short accounts and forgiving quickly helps keep our roots healthy and deep in God's love. And His grace will keep us just as He preserved the little peach tree and sustained Flo through that stormy, trying period of her life.

7. *Look at problems as opportunities.* Problems are inevitable. Just because you have them doesn't mean you've missed God's will. Look at Daniel, Elijah, John the Baptist, and Paul and the problems they faced! Problems give us tremendous opportunities to grow, to stretch our faith, and to depend on God in a greater way. They cause our roots to go down deeper in Christ. Sometimes difficulties on the journey cause us to reevaluate, which can be useful. But we are hopeful they won't cause us to turn back or give up on the adventure of following God.

If you can find a path with no obstacles,
it probably doesn't lead anywhere.
—Frank A. Clark

For almost every dream, idea, or goal God gives us, there is a delay, a time of difficulty, and even a dead end in which our situation deteriorates from difficult to impossible and it looks hopeless for us to accomplish our goal. But these times are sent for a special purpose.[3] Paul said he and the brothers were crushed and overwhelmed in Asia, burdened beyond their strength, and even told themselves that it was the end. He went on to say that they had this sense of impending disaster so that "we should not trust in ourselves, but in God who raises the dead; who delivered us from so great a peril of death, and will deliver us, He on whom we have set our hope" (2 Cor. 1:9–10, NASB).

Even in the midst of the problems, we can find peace on the trail. It all depends on our perspective. Catherine Marshall told of a friend who had boarded a plane and was waiting for takeoff. As she settled into her seat and buckled her seatbelt, she noticed a strange thing. On one side of the airplane a sunset filled the entire sky with glorious color. But out of the window next to her seat, all she could see was a dark, threatening sky, with no sign of the beautiful sunset.

As the plane began to take off, a gentle Voice spoke within her: You have noticed the windows. Your life, too, will contain some happy, beautiful times, but also some dark shadows. Here's a lesson I want to teach you to save you much heartache and allow you to abide in Me with continual peace and joy.

You see, it doesn't matter which window you look through; this plane is still going to Cleveland. So it is in your life. You have a choice. You can dwell on the gloomy picture. Or you can focus on the bright things and leave the dark, ominous situations to Me. I alone can handle them anyway.

And the final destination is not influenced by what you see or feel along the way. If we learn this, we will be released and able to experience the peace that passes understanding on our Adventure through life.[4]

8. *Don't put off joy.* If we're always thinking we'll be happy when we lose those ten pounds or when our child gets potty-trained or through adolescence or we get the right job or meet our goals—that day may never come. Don't miss out on joy *today.* Speak to your soul each morning and say, "This is the

day the Lord has made. I will rejoice and be glad in it" (Ps. 118:24).

Then remind yourself throughout the day to celebrate. I have a card on my bathroom mirror that says, "Celebrate today! I have come that you might have life abundantly!" It reminds me on the darkest days to find something to celebrate: a gorgeous Oklahoma sunset, a daffodil peeking up after a cold winter, a letter from a friend. Each day is a gift, and there's always something to celebrate!

One of my favorite poems of William Wordsworth begins, "My heart leaps up when I behold a rainbow in the sky. So was it when I was a child, so be it when I am a man, or let me die." What makes your heart leap up? Seek it out:

- If it's flowers, go to a rose garden, or if it's beautiful paintings, head for an art museum when you have some time off.

- Make time to swing with your toddler at the park and laugh in the wind.

- Take a walk. Exercise is not only a great stress-reducer and one of the best remedies for anxiety, but it gives you a chance to find something to celebrate!

- Look for the miraculous in your everyday life: the miracle of a sunrise, a new baby, even an angelic visitation. Whatever simple pleasure you find in nature or the world around you, let your heart leap up, and you'll be filled with wonder instead of worry. Remember, when we cease to wonder, we cease to worship!

Peggy, a nurse and mother of three, has gone on three medical mission trips to Mexico and the Amazon River. She teaches CPR classes for the American Red Cross and sets up first aid stations in the community. In her spare time she serves as an animal educator, showing zoo animals to schoolchildren, giving special tours at the zoos, and teaching classes about animals. For ten years she served each summer as a camp nurse for two hundred children in a camp. At forty-nine years old, she tackled rock climbing and goes on regular mountain climbing and hiking adventures with the Sierra Club. What is her secret to living an adventurous life?

"The size of your world is the size of your heart" is a poster Peggy looks at every morning on her closet door. She's found her heart is happiest learning, exploring, and "out on the range." This former psychiatric nurse who once launched a clown ministry with her youth group says there are always more places to explore and things she wants to do. Two other posters right by her breakfast table say "Carpe Diem!" (Seize the Day) and "If life isn't an adventure, it's not living at all." These are visual reminders—like a breath of fresh air—for her to look for miracles, try something new, and grow!

In this life we need not carry
our own burdens; the Lord is our
burden-bearer, and on Him we can
lay every care.
—*Hannah Whitall Smith*

9. *Keep casting all your cares and anxieties upon the Lord daily, because He cares for you* (see 1 Pet. 5:7). If you don't, you'll be too burdened down to continue on the Adventure trail, or you'll get weary and drop out or burn out. God wants us to soar like the eagles and run with the horses, but we won't have the physical or spiritual energy to keep up with Him if we're carrying a fifty-pound burden of worry on our backs.

When Carol came out of an abusive marriage ten years ago, she had so much fear and anxiety. "I was into crisis-living," says Carol. She just *knew* her tires were going to fall off her old car. She dreaded the first of the month rolling around, afraid she couldn't pay the bills. When she heard sirens, she just knew her teenage daughter was in a wreck.

Finally, exhausted and burned out, Carol said, "No more. I can't live this way." She began to realize God meant what He said about being anxious for *nothing*: "Make your requests known, and He will take care of them all" (see Phil. 4:6). She began to continually roll her burdens over on God in prayer and to stay close to Him. In doing so, her energy began to be renewed, and she started her own business. Eventually she was able to support herself and her daughter, even send her to college, and to help other people as well.

When you're doing your work and using your gifts for God's service, it is easy to think you have to carry the whole responsibility for the work yourself and worry that the results will please Him. But that's when it's crucial to cast your cares upon Him! "But if the work is Christ's, the responsibility is His also, and we have no need to worry about results," says Hannah Whitall Smith. "The most effectual workers I know are those who do not feel the least anxiety about their work, but who commit it all to their Master. They ask Him to guide them moment by moment and trust Him implicitly for each moment's supply of wisdom and strength."[5]

10. *Remember, God promises that no matter what happens on the Adventure, nothing can separate us from His love*: "For I am convinced that neither death nor life, neither angels nor demons, neither the present nor the future, nor any powers, neither height, nor depth, nor any thing else in all creation, will be able to separate us from the love of God, which is in Christ Jesus our Lord" (Rom. 8:38–39).

No matter what difficulties happen on the journey—regardless of whether you find success or failure (by the world's standards) in your pursuit of your mission or in using your talents—God couldn't love you any more than He does right now, and He'll never quit loving you. He loved you so much He gave Himself totally to you and asks that you respond to His love. When you do commit yourself to living the Adventure of following Christ, your life will be woven into God's plan not only in this life, but for all eternity!

As I wrap up this book, Holmes and I are facing many uncertainties that could be cause for worry. Will I never have a fearful thought again? Will the panic button never get pushed? Will I always be cool as a cucumber in the face of danger? Doubtful! But when circumstances get shaky and anxiety starts to rise, I've learned that fear can be the springboard to jump into God's arms, to run to His presence. That's when my worry can be turned to wonder because I know where to go with it! We have a refuge—a heavenly Father who wants us to cast our cares upon Him day by day, a Savior who'll never leave us or forsake us, and a Holy Spirit whom God has sent to comfort and guide us in all the real stuff of life. And nothing, no problem or crisis, can separate us from His love.

I pray that His love will be your anchor as you are willing to take risks and say yes to God—boldly and prayerfully, acknowledging God in all your ways (see Prov. 3:4–5) and following the light He has put on your path. And the Adventure of knowing and serving Him will never end.

Thank You, Father,
that You are rest for the weary,
peace for the storm-tossed,
strength for the powerless,
and wisdom for all those who ask You.
You are exceedingly abundantly beyond
all we can ask or think—of blessing, help, and care.

Questions for Discussion and Reflection

Anxiety, fear, and worry are particularly good topics to deal with in a group setting for several reasons: Often the anxious person feels she is the only one who struggles with fear. When she finds that others have similar worries, there's a great sense of relief. In addition, when problems or burdens we carry alone are "divided," their sting is lessened by having others to discuss them and pray with us.

The material in this book lends itself to discussing and studying with a group, so questions are provided here for group discussion. They are also ideal for individual reflection and journaling. The questions will help the reader or group participant move from the abstract to the concrete, from just thinking about fear and worry to taking action. In doing so, she will move from fear to faith, from worry to wonder. Have a notebook and Bible handy as you interact with one another, with the material, and with God.

Introduction

1. What previous or present experience keeps you from putting complete trust in God?

2. Are there unsolved issues from your childhood that keep resurfacing in your life? If so, name them.

3. What present fear (or fears) tends to paralyze you in your faith?

4. Reread "The High Cost of Fear"and pray for God to give you a proper perspective on your own fear and the ability to trust Him with it.

Chapter One

1. What adventure do you feel God is leading you into?

2. What keeps you from going forward into this adventure?

3. Find a particular Scripture to encourage you. Write it on a three-by-five-inch-card and tape it on your kitchen cabinet or bathroom mirror. Memorize it so you will have it with you everywhere you go.

4. Share about a time you offered yourself to God as Romans 12:1 suggests, stepped out in faith, and He worked through you or used you in His purpose.

5. Is there a burden you are carrying or an area of your life in which you would like to experience more peace and less anxiety?

Chapter Two

1. As a parent, is it hard for you to believe that God loves your child more than you do?

2. Are you afraid to relinquish your child to God? If so, pray that He will reveal where this fear comes from and give you the faith to trust Him with your child.

3. Think about how faithful God has been in your life and your children's lives in the past and discuss some blessings you can give thanks for, some specific things He has done. When you are gripped by anxiety about your children, sit down and

write all of God's past goodness to your family you can remember.

4. What does Isaiah 26:3 say about the benefits of turning your thoughts to God and His Word? After making your own Peace Packet and using it on a daily basis as suggested in this chapter, share with the group your results.

5. Share about a time that you experienced fear or worry in regard to your child: a crisis occurred, you had to take him to the emergency room, or his well-being was threatened. How did you respond? What can you do when these kinds of things happen in the future?

6. Pray some of the Scripture promises ("Lifesavers and Worrybusters") that accompany this chapter, putting your child's name in the verses.

Chapter Three

1. Are all of your financial worries real or are you borrowing some of tomorrow's problems?

2. Proverbs 11:14 says, "Where there is no guidance, the people fall / But in abundance of counselors there is victory" (NASB). Confide in someone you trust if you need counsel or discernment with a financial problem and pray about the problem.

3. What is the difference between walking through a time of financial difficulty and trial in trembling anxiety and with trust in God?

4. Ask God to be your partner in making a budget and sticking with it. Then memorize Scripture that reinforces God's goodness and His desire for good in your life.

5. Has the financial "rug" ever been pulled out from under you, or has money been so tight you didn't know how you were going to meet your family's needs and pay all the bills? Share about how God provided and turned your worry to wonder.

6. Practice the gift of giving. Think of something to give to someone this week. It may be cookies, baby-sitting, flowers, or even an encouraging word, but give *something* away. You

will bless yourself and someone else. Share with your group what you gave and the results.

Chapter Four

1. Discuss the quote, "Fear is the handle by which we lay hold of God." When did your fear of people or rejection or anxiety about a relationship become the means to your running *to* God instead of *away from* what you feared and thus helped you begin to overcome the fear?

2. Write down on a sheet of paper any bitterness or resentment you harbor toward your mate or some other person. Pray over the list, asking God's forgiveness and for the ability to let go. When you feel a release, thank God for His faithfulness, then burn the sheet of paper as a sign of your forgiveness to the other person or persons.

3. What is your greatest need today? Practice praying the names of God. Choose the name of God that covers that particular need. (For example, if your greatest need is healing, He is Jehovah-Rapha, the God Who Heals; if it is peace, He is Jehovah-Shalom, the God of Peace.) Thank Him for His sufficiency and pray fervently.

4. When circumstances overwhelm you, one of the best things to do is look for someone in the Bible who went through something similar. (David fought a giant; Daniel was delivered from lions and his enemies; Ruth lost her husband and left her home, put her grief aside, and cared for her mother-in-law, etc.) Discuss the biblical character who went through a trial similar to what you are presently going through. What can you learn from his or her experience?

5. Read aloud a psalm. What does it reveal about how God loves and cares for His people? What does it say about the benefits of trusting and relying upon Him?

6. Is there a "blizzard" or storm in your life that has enabled you to learn something new about God's character or love for you?

Chapter Five

1. What fear keeps you from "flying" in life's great adventure?

2. What "high place" do you feel God wants to take you to? If you don't know, ask Him.

3. Is it hard to give control of your life to God? If so, meditate on Psalm 139. Remember that God is the One who knows and ordained the number of your days.

4. Someone said that without having our own "resurrection" experience with Christ, we become frantic people who dance faster and work harder to contain our fright. Share about a life-changing experience you had that gave you hope for the future and increased your faith in God.

5. One of the most encouraging words in Scripture is "And surely I will be with you always, to the very end of the age" (Matt. 28:20). What does this mean in terms of our facing, with God's presence and power, any situation or trial that might be ahead?

Chapter Six

1. What were some of your childhood fears that may have gotten dragged into adulthood?

2. How did you react when you were young and afraid of something? Did you withdraw, go for help to your parents, or have another response? How do you react today when something frightens you?

3. Can you identify the cause of your greatest anxiety? Do you know why it has a grip on your life?

4. How has your adult life been affected by childhood fears or fears you've acquired along the journey that you continue to carry?

5. Can you lay these fears down at the foot of the cross and ask God for freedom and newness of life? Your group can designate a "God Box" for each person to write down individual fears and leave in the box as an outward sign of trusting God in that area.

Chapter Seven

1. What pushes your "panic button"?

2. Where do you turn when panic or worry strikes you?

3. The next time you panic, write down your thoughts, what is happening to you at that time, and how you are responding in the situation. Do this each time you become extremely anxious to see if you can find a pattern, or "trigger," for your panic.

4. What are one or two areas of your life that God is calling you to bring under the shadow of His wing and stop worrying about?

5. Share about a time God spoke to you in a trial or stormy season of your life that brought calm and peace to your heart and mind.

6. Memorize Philippians 4:6–9 and practice the Five P's the next time a worry or anxiety-producing situation hits your life.

Chapter Eight

1. Have you discovered a talent that God has given you, a gift you've been hiding under a bushel that God wants you to develop and use? Write it down and share it with the group. How are you using the gifts God gave you?

2. What activities or challenges do you fear and avoid whenever possible?

3. Do you have a desire to do something more but fear you aren't good enough and might fail? Write out your desire and ask God if this is from Him. If so, go for it!

4. Has the fear of failure ever held you back from following through with a project or mission God had led you into? How can the fear of failure paralyze our talents and gifts?

5. Review the "Bringing It Home" suggestions and share your responses with the group or with a trusted friend. What passion or burning desire has God put in your heart to do at this time of your life?

Chapter Nine

1. Are you living in traumatic or "uncontrollable" circumstances? Name them. Do you see any way out of your situation?

2. Do you wonder if God really loves you and cares about your circumstances? Immerse yourself in Scripture where you'll be reminded over and over that:

- God has good plans for your life and future.
- God hears your cry and your prayers.
- God is always with you and will not desert you.
- God is your protector, your Hiding Place, and your refuge—He wants you to run to Him!
- God promises you mercy and comfort.
- God will empower and equip you for whatever you will face.

3. Tell God your fears, frustrations, and anger and ask for peace. Ask others to pray for you, then ask God to help you trust and believe in His goodness.

4. Where are some stories in Scripture that tell of people in difficult circumstances—people who had bad things happen to them—who praised God and trusted Him in the midst of their trials? Praise God for His faithfulness, even in the middle of your circumstances.

5. Is someone needier or lonelier than you are whom you could reach out to and serve even while you're in a troubling time?

Chapter Ten

1. Is there a particular illness that you fear because it seems to run in your family?

2. Do you take care of your body with exercise, proper nutrition, and plenty of rest to help avoid illness?

3. Are you wondering why God allowed a particular illness?

4. Pray to the Great Healer—Jehovah-Rapha. Pour out your heart. Ask for healing of your body, mind, emotions, and spirit, and then praise God for His healing.

5. Did the experiences of Nancy, Kathy, or any of the women recovering from illness remind you of a time in your life when God was working or when you were learning something that you were later able to comfort another person with?

6. How can anxiety and fear make illness or physical conditions worse? Write down three ways you can cope with the anxiety that is generated by being diagnosed with a disease or illness.

Chapter Eleven

1. This chapter is entitled "Acceptance: The Door to Peace." What is a situation that produced increased peace and reliance on God when you came into acceptance?

2. Write out and share the difference between acceptance of an individual and acceptance of a behavior.

3. Are you experiencing a difficult circumstance that you see no change in and can't control? Is it difficult to pray or read your Bible? Call on another member of the group as a prayer partner or a staff member in your church for this particular situation.

4. Have you ever felt like Marilyn did when she reviewed all the unanswered prayers she'd prayed? Describe a time you couldn't sense God's love or help and felt frustrated. What turned the situation or your attitude around?

5. What steps can you take to move toward acceptance in a present trial?

6. Is it possible, as Fenelon says, "If you recognize the hand of God, and make no opposition to His will, [to] have peace (and even joy) in the midst of affliction"? Share about a unique set of circumstances you've experienced that you were certain was from God and in which you eventually found joy.

Chapter Twelve

1. How can a lifestyle of praise turn worry to wonder?

2. Is your spirit low? Then make the choice to praise with songs and psalms. It's a great antidote.

3. Give something to someone when you feel you have nothing to give. It will help you rejoice.

4. Is there someone in your life like Anne the missionary or a spiritual mentor who, by her example and wisdom, has encouraged you to praise God even when you didn't feel like it?

5. First Thessalonians 5:18 says, "In everything give thanks." Write out a prayer of praise and thanksgiving to God, including how you see Him working in your present circumstances. If desired, share this praise with your group or a close friend.

Chapter Thirteen

1. Make your own list of the step or steps God has shown you to take when He has put light on your path and guided you. When you took a step of faith, what was the result? How did He meet you?

2. Are you actively pursuing an adventure with God, moving out of your comfort zone to follow His leading?

3. When has your journey been plagued by fear and worry? What was God teaching you? What lesson did you learn?

4. Share about a time when a problem became an opportunity, when God redeemed one of your mistakes, or when what looked like a failure was turned into something beautiful that God used in His tapestry for good.

5. Look for joy in people and simple, everyday things. Share with your group or write in your journal ten or more things to celebrate and enjoy *today*.

6. Remember that you are God's child, and nothing can separate you from His love!

Endnotes

Introduction

1. Denise F. Beckfield, *Master Your Panic* (San Luis Obispo, Calif.: Impact Publishers, 1994).

2. Keith Miller and Bruce Larsen, *The Edge of Adventure: An Experiment in Faith* (Waco, Tex.: Word Books Publisher, 1976), 180.

3. Ibid.

Chapter 3

1. Pamela Reeve, *Faith Is* (Sisters, Oreg.: Multnomah Books, 1994), 22.

Chapter 4

1. Bruce Larsen, *Living Beyond Our Fears* (New York: Harper & Row Publishers, 1990), 128.

2. Ibid., 150.

3. The term "Christ-conscious" is adapted from Larsen, *Living Beyond Our Fears*, 131.

4. A. W. Tozer, *The Pursuit of God* (Camp Hill, Pa.: Christian Publications, Inc., 1982), 91.

5. "Arms of Love," Mercy Publishing, ©1991.

6. A. W. Tozer, *Whatever Happened to Worship?* (Camp Hill, Pa.: Christian Publications, Inc., 1985), 67.

Chapter 5

1. Dale Carnegie, *The Quick and Easy Way to Effective Speaking* (New York: Dale Carnegie & Associates, 1985), 27.

2. Hannah Hurnard, *Hinds' Feet on High Places* (Wheaton, Ill.: Tyndale House Publishers, 1975), 17.

3. Ibid.

4. Elisabeth Elliot, *Keep a Quiet Heart* (Ann Arbor, Mich.: Servant Publications, 1995), 53.

Chapter 6

1. Robert S. McGee, *The Search for Freedom* (Ann Arbor, Mich.: Servant Publications, 1995), 65.

2. Ibid.

Chapter 7

1. Robert Jamieson, quoted in Cynthia Heald's *Abiding in Christ* (Colorado Springs: NavPress, 1995), 44.

Chapter 8

1. Ellen Hawkes, "I'm Still Searching," *Parade Magazine*, March 10, 1996, 6.

2. Reported in "Air Born" by Robert L. Crandall, "Vantage Point," *American Way*, May 1, 1994, 8.

3. Dale Carnegie, *The Quick and Easy Way to Effective Speaking* (Garden City, N.Y.: Dale Carnegie & Associates, Inc., 1985), 26.

4. Ibid.

Chapter 9

1. Larry Jones, "Controlling the Uncontrollable," (Oklahoma City: Feed the Children, 1995), 2.

2. Amy Carmichael, *Edges of His Ways* (Fort Washington, Pa.: Christian Literature Crusade, 1988), 175.

3. M. Scott Peck, *The Road Less Travelled* (San Franscisco: Touchstone Books, 1980).

4. From Cathy Herndon's "Peace Packet" (Oklahoma City, Okla., 1995), 12.

5. Don Gossett, *How to Conquer Fear* (Springdale, Pa.: Whitaker House, 1981), 86–87.

Chapter 11

1. Hannah Hurnard, *Hinds' Feet in High Places* (Wheaton, Ill.: Tyndale House Publishers, 1975), 11–12.

2. Fenelon, *Let Go* (Springdale, Pa.: Whitaker House, 1973), 3.

3. David Wilkerson, "Bringing Christ into Your Crisis," Times Square Church Pulpit Series, January 1, 1996, 4.

Chapter 12

1. Ruth Myers, *31 Days of Praise* (Singapore: The Navigators, 1992).

2. Ibid., 19.

3. Fern Nichols, "Heart to Heart," vol. 7, no. 4 (1995): 1.

Chapter 13

1. Keith Miller and Bruce Larsen, *The Edge of Adventure: An Experiment in Faith* (Waco, Tex.: Word Books, 1976), 64.

2. A. W. Tozer, *The Pursuit of God* (Camp Hill, Pa.: Christian Publications, Inc., 1982), 82.

3. Rick Warren, *Fax of Life* (Mission Viejo, Calif., self-published, January 6, 1996).

4. Catherine Marshall in *Touching the Heart of God*, quoted in *Christianity Today*, May 15, 1995, 36.

5. Hannah Whitall Smith, *God Is Enough* (New York: Ballantine Books, 1986), 103.